ST JOHN OF THE CROSS

Edited by Peter Slattery

ST JOHN OF THE CROSS
A spirituality of substance

ALBA·HOUSE   NEW·YORK

SOCIETY OF ST. PAUL, 2187 VICTORY BLVD., STATEN ISLAND, NEW YORK 10314

ST JOHN OF THE CROSS: A spirituality of substance
© Peter Slattery O.Carm. (ed)

First published, July 1994

Cover painting: Luciano Morandi
Cover design & photo: Bruno Colombari SSP

AUSTRALIAN EDITION
Published by
ST PAULS – Society of St Paul,
60-70 Broughton Road – (PO Box 230) – Homebush, NSW 2140

National Library of Australia
Cataloguing-in-Publication data:
St John of the Cross: a spirituality of substance.
ISBN 1 875570 36 5
1. John, of the Cross, Saint, 1542-1591 – Congresses. 2. Spirituality – Catholic Church
– Congresses. 3. Spiritual life – Catholic Church – Congresses. 4. Prayer – Catholic Church
– Congresses. I. Slattery, Peter.
248.42

NORTH AMERICAN EDITION
Published by
ALBA HOUSE – Society of St Paul,
2187 Victory Boulevard, Staten Island, New York, 10314-6603
ISBN 0-8189-0684-7

ST PAULS and ALBA HOUSE are activities of the Priests and Brothers of the Society of St Paul who proclaim the Gospel through the media of social communication.

ACKNOWLEDGEMENTS

- Extracts taken from:

The Collected Works of St John of the Cross, translated by Kieran Kavanaugh and Otilio Rodriguez © 1979 by Washington Province of Discalced Carmelites. ICS Publications, 2131 Lincoln Rd, N.E. Washington D.C. 2002 USA.

The Complete Works of St John of the Cross, E. Allison Peers, trans and ed, Burns & Oates, Tunbridge Wells, Kent, UK, 1974.

Walking Side by Side with All Men and Women, St John of the Cross, A Letter from the Council of the Carmelite Order to its members, Institutum Carmelitanum, Rome, 1991.

Meditating Day and Night on the Law of the Lord and Keeping Vigil in Prayer, Carlos Mesters, in *Carmelite 9*, 1991.

Resonant Silences, Ross Collings, in *Eureka Street*, Jesuit Publications, Richmond, Victoria, 1991.

Burnt Norton V Four Quartets, T.S. Eliot, Faber & Faber, London.

A Theological Aesthetics, Vol 1, Seeing the Form, in *The Glory of the Lord*, Hans Urs von Balthasar, T & T Clark, Edinburgh, 1982.

Meister Eckhart, Edward College and Bernard McGinn, trans and intro, Paulist Press, New York, 1981.

Eckhart's Way, Richard Woods, Michael Glazier, Delaware, NJ, 1986.

On Christian Faith, The Spiritual, Ethical and Political Dimensions, Edward Schillebeeckx, Crossroad, New York, 1987.

Beyond Anger, Carolyn Osiek, Paulist Press, New York, 1986.

Master in Faith, John Paul II, Institutum Carmelitanum, Rome, 1991.

A Sleep of Prisoners, Christopher Fry, Oxford University Press, England, 1951.

• All used by permission of the Publishers.

CONTRIBUTORS

Veronica Brady IBVM, *a member of the Institute of the Blessed Virgin Mary (Loreto Sisters), is Associate Professor of English at the University of Western Australia.*

Gregory Burke OCD, *a Discalced Carmelite friar, was Parish Priest of the Infant of Jesus Parish, Morley, Western Australia, now lives in St Teresa's Monastery, Brisbane.*

John Follent OCD, *a Discalced Carmelite friar, is Lecturer in the Department of Systematic Theology at the Yarra Theological Union, Box Hill, Victoria.*

Brian Pitman O.Carm., *a Carmelite friar, is Chaplain at St Anne's Hospital, Mount Lawley, Western Australia.*

Peter Slattery O.Carm., *a Carmelite friar, is Director of the Carmelite Centre, Middle Park, Victoria.*

Placid Spearritt OSB, *a Benedictine monk, is the Prior Administrator of Holy Trinity Abbey, New Norcia, Western Australia.*

Sonia Wagner SGS, *a Good Samaritan sister, was the Director of Pastoral Planning, the Archdiocese of Perth, Western Australia, now Congregational Leader of the Good Samaritan Sisters and lives in Glebe, NSW.*

John Welch O.Carm., *a Carmelite friar, is Lecturer in Spiritual Theology, the Washington Theological Union, Washington DC, USA.*

CONTENTS

INTRODUCTION

The chapters in this book discuss many of the social and personal issues which men and women of good faith confront today and will face more and more in the future. In one way or another the different authors turn to one of the greatest mystics of the Christian tradition, St John of the Cross, to seek help for developing a spirituality for the future in the challenges of the next century – *a spirituality of substance*.

The chapters were first presented as papers at a conference in Perth, Western Australia, from December 11-13, 1991 to celebrate the 4th Centenary of the death of St John of the Cross. The Carmelite and the Discalced Carmelite friars wanted to present something worthwhile to the local church, not only to mark this occasion, but as a contribution to the ongoing search of many men and women for a richer and more meaningful spiritual life.

The attendance at this three-day conference indicated that there are many on this spiritual quest, thus encouraging us to publish these contributions in book form.

Peter Slattery

Peter Slattery O.Carm.

NAMING OUR FUTURE

Among many ancient peoples there is a hesitancy to reveal one's name and usually only pseudonyms and descriptive names are used. A person's real name is known only by intimate members of one's family, and this is because to know one's name is to know one's very essence and, consequently, to have power over that person. This is similar to the hesitation of the Hebrew people to name God and to use instead descriptions such as El Shaddai.

It is in this sense that 'naming' is used as an active, ongoing exercise which helps us to create our future imaginatively, rather than be passive recipients of the future controlled and handed on by others. The title of this chapter contains the collective word 'our', because the future is a communal experience and cannot be privatised by the 'me-generation' of the sixties and seventies. The title also talks about the future. While it is true, in one sense, that we cannot know the future, in another sense, we pass on to the next generation what we have created in our past and present. So the title implies that we are challenged to take the power of our lives and our communities creatively so that what we hand on to the next generation is worthwhile, safe, hopeful – it also implies that those of us in the field of educating for spirituality can assist men and women to share the task of naming our future.

To be able to name the future we have to name the present. However, as we shall see, we have some competition about naming the present: who names the present and how do we identify where we are and where we should go.

We shall look at a theological response at attempts to name the present, so that as a community we are in a better position to name our future. We shall look at the mystic, St John of the Cross, to help us enunciate both a spirituality of substance and a spirituality for the future.

1. NAMING THE PRESENT

The paradigm shifts of the past from the cosmology of the Hebrews to Copernicus

Imagine what it would be like if you were a person who believed in the cosmology of the Hebrews, when Copernicus tells you that the earth is not flat but round, and the earth is not in the centre of things, but on the periphery of the sun among other planets.

That is what it would be like to live through a paradigm shift – a total change in your world view, a challenge to all your beliefs and attitudes, a destabilising of the way you see God, your fellow human persons, yourself and many other things.

Many commentators, writers and researchers in many fields and disciplines from physics, science, technology, to philosophy, sociology, anthropology, to art, literature and music, are saying that we are now living through a massive paradigm shift, the proportions of which are as great as the shift from Hebrew cosmology to that of Copernicus. It is the view of many of these theorists that we are fairly sure from what we are moving, but are not very clear where we are going, or with what we will end up.

The world view of the Age of the Enlightenment

The Enlightenment presented a philosophy of the human person as triumphant, self-confident, self-fulfilling, self-actualising with no need for a God who both loves and liberates. The Enlightenment made the middle class male of western Europe the centre of the universe — thus, one's cosmology had a centre and all other things and people were measured by this centre, and named accordingly. Therefore, you still hear the terms 'The Near East' and 'The Far East' — near to whom? Far from what?

The Enlightenment man saw the universe as triumphant in the world of science, which could explain everything with no need for a God, with no need for the death and resurrection of Christ who liberates human people from the destruction of their own evil. Patrick White's *Voss* raises the question of the God of this ancient continent. Voss is a self-confident, self-reliant man of the European Enlightenment, having a contempt for God because he is not made in Voss's image and likeness. Voss is humbled by his sufferings in the Australian desert, learning that to be human is to be vulnerable. Yet it is only when he comes

to this understanding that he accepts the need for salvation
and liberation. Then he sees God not in splendour, but as
the crucified person who has been crucified and killed by
the evil forces of this world.

When God becomes a person, in the eyes of Voss, he
rejects the establishment notion of the human person and
he (Voss) takes his place with those who are powerless, cast
out, and poor.[1] The way you look at the world affects
many of your beliefs, even the way you see God.

Conflicting and competitive attempts at naming the present

David Tracy has shown that we are in the throes of a
paradigm shift, and that there are at least three conflicting
attempts to name the present. These are typified by what
he calls the moderns, the anti-moderns and the post-
moderns — all three are now competing for our allegiance.[2]

For some the present is still the age of modernity and
the triumph of the bourgeoisie. Positivist technology has
been produced by the age of science and the leitmotif for
the modern is: develop and consume or bust.

This can be heard when the economic rationalists want
to describe the whole life and universe in terms of produc-
tion and supply. The moderns want to continue to propa-
gate the triumph of science and the age of reason.

1   Veronica Brady, *A Crucible of Prophets* Theological Explorations,
    Sydney, 1981.
2   David Tracy, *Plurality and Ambiguity: Hermeneutics, Religion, Hope*,
    Harper & Row, San Francisco, 1987.

For the anti-moderns we are in the age of the collapse of the overconfident, and we await the return of the repressed traditions that were swept away by the liberal revolutions of the 18th and 19th centuries. The clearest and most startling expression of this anti-modern stance is fundamentalism. We can see this expression in Moslem fundamentalism of the Ayatollahs of Iran, the rise of Hindu fundamentalism in India, and the rise of all sorts of Christian fundamentalism throughout the Christian world. All these have a suspicion of the achievements of western rationalism and have become ahistorical in their efforts to find simple and definite answers to the complexities of the universe. Among the anti-moderns could be gathered the various neo-conservative groups, who are suspicious of the age of the Enlightenment and are highly selective in their approach to history and tradition. Many neo-conservatives would be happy to return to what it was like just before the Enlightenment.

For the post-moderns we are in a present that has witnessed the passing of modernity – the passing of the ascendancy of western humanity and its efforts to structure all things similar to science and reason. The post-moderns are moving from the premisses of the Enlightenment, for the most part, with one or all of the following critiques:

The environmental critique
The feminist critique
The universal call for justice.

The environmental critique

A telling critique of the Enlightenment Age of Reason is the post-modern concern about the environment in which we live. This has been prompted, in part, by a huge change in understanding science and technology. For nearly three hundred years this understanding was dominated by Newtonian physics which perceived the universe as if it were a machine, and later came the thermodynamic paradigm of a degenerating universe – the machine running down. Now there is a new paradigm explained by such physicists as Stephen Hawking[3] and Paul Davies[4] as an emerging universe or a self re-creating universe.

This has encouraged a new interest in the blessing of creation with the writings of Thomas Berry and Matthew Fox.[5] They have made us more aware of the gift of creation, the goodness of the earth, which offers us life. Instead of seeing human beings like factory managers of a big machine, we are called to co-operate as co-creators with God and live in peace and harmony with the whole of the universe.

This implies a need to reject the values and the attitudes arising from paradigms of the past – values like exploitation, over-development and competition, and adopt harmonious and co-operative means of sustaining life on this planet for the benefit of all.

This critique challenges humans to achieve ecological sustainability instead of continuing with the dictums of the economic rationalists to develop more and consume more. This critique maintains that to continually dig up more

3   Stephen Hawking, *A Brief History of Time; From Big Bang to Black Holes*. Bantam Press, London, 1968.
4   Paul Davies, *God and the New Physics*. Simon & Schuster, New York, 1983.
5   *For examples of their writings see:* Thomas Berry, *Cross Currents*, 37, (Summer/Fall) 1987, 273 pp. 178-224; Matthew Fox, *Original Blessing: A Primer in Creation Spirituality*. Bear & Co, Santa Fe, NM, 1983.

minerals, chop down more trees, guzzle more oil will simply make life on this planet impossible. The 1987 Report of the World Commission on Environment and Development: *Our Common Future* urges substantial changes relating to the world economy and ecology.

We need to work harmoniously together to create a sustainable agriculture, forestry, fisheries, manufacturing, tourism and energy use. We need to live in a very connected way with the emerging universe.

The feminist critique

A second post-modern critique is that of the feminists. Many women today are breaking open the silence in which their lives have been shrouded for generations. They are beginning to name their new sense of themselves, of the world, of God, of their own Godlikeness.

Their experience is characterised by connectedness – a notion that perceives reality wholistically, organically and intimately related. A new wisdom literature is being developed as women tell their stories and share their experience.

They have shown how much of the Enlightenment thinking was that of white, European, middle class men, done from a rationalist, instrumental and utilitarian background. They have documented women's exclusion from the development of the theoretical constructs of the recent past, and from the ranks of those who shaped the symbols of our civilisation.

Women's writings and enquiries have re-emphasised the passionate God of the incarnation, imagination, resistance, and solidarity.

Rosemary Haughton,[6] for example, has written about the reclaiming of the holiness of our inspirited bodies and the gift of passion as a force to move us onwards. She writes of the eros at the heart of human history that drives 'the minds and hearts made for wisdom, for the Wise Word that would set them free'.

The recent investigations of women have helped us to draw more deeply on the power of imagination, to develop symbols that mirror a more inclusive experience of reality and meaning.

Again, Haughton suggests that if the symbol of Eve was used by a male-dominated culture to indicate 'women's innate sinfulness, her power to degrade and corrupt', then Jesus' empowerment of women could be described as the 're-creation of Eve'.

Inherent in such writing and thinking is a resistance – a refusal to accept unquestioningly, as reflecting universal human experience, the definitions, doctrines, world views, prohibitions and patterns created by men.

The feminist critique is also characterised by solidarity – the reclaiming of community. Women's experiences of exclusion link them with all who experience oppression and injustice.

The image of connection describes women's commitment to relational ways of knowing, living, acting and praying. One author finds that the quest for wholeness, the understanding of everything as intrinsically interrelated, is characteristic of women's way of knowing.[7]

6   Rosemary Haughton, *The Passionate God*. Paulist, New York, 1981.
7   Patricia Wilson-Kastner, *Faith, Feminism and Christ*. Fortress, Philadelphia, 1983, p. 19.

The universal call for justice

Another post-modern critique of the Enlightenment is the universal call for justice. This is a demand from the have-nots for a just use of the resources of the world and an equitable share in the wealth of creation.

Many people of the world reject both the capitalism and communism that has condemned them to grinding poverty, exploitation, homelessness, periodic famine, and lack of adequate housing, education and standards of living. Many refuse to accept the rationalistic consumerism, and the materialist planned economies which create the greenhouse effect, acid rain, rain forest depletion and desertification.

The so-called third world countries and those emerging from communism want a just share in the world's resources and wealth. They are joined by those throughout the world who are homeless, hungry and humiliated by bigotry, racism, nationalism and gender intolerance. A new paradigm of co-operative globalism is being called for, so that men and women can share equitably in the goods and benefits of life.

These post-modern critiques of the principles of the Enlightenment move us into the middle of a massive paradigm shift – and as we stand we are not sure where it will lead us. Because we are in this situation I would like to reflect on a theological response.

2. A THEOLOGICAL RESPONSE

Considering all this, what is the response of the theologians? Many theologians start from the following premisses:

(a) all creation is created by God and is good;
(b) men and women are created in the image and likeness of God.
(c) throughout all paradigm shifts, from Hebrew times until the present time, the Spirit of God survives, the Word of God and the message and values of Jesus continue to be heard in the hearts and spirits of people in the world.

In the light of the competitive naming of the present, in the marketplace of ideas and theories where so many are seeking our allegiance, theologians advise the baptised Christian to take:

A mythical-prophetic stance of resistance and hope[8]

Tracy says that to get a full theological Christian naming of the present we must listen to other conversations, especially those of people in our own and other cultures who experience massive global suffering but have found new voices of their own and new historical actions to match those voices. He says that part of what one can hear in the voices of the 'others', is the healing and the transforming message of the Christian gospel alive once again: a message neither modern, nor anti-modern, nor post-modern; a message to and for historical subjects in the concrete struggles for justice against suffering and oppression and for total liberation (p. 80).

Mystic: The mystics are men and women filled and enamoured with and enraptured by the Spirit of God; men

8   David Tracy, On Naming the Present, *Concilium*, 1, 1990, pp. 66-85.

and women dedicated to all that is great in the human spirit
— art, music, literature, science, technology, etc. Contemplatives are men and women fully human and fully divine
in the sense of St Irenaeus, who can take a 'long, loving
look at the real'.

Prophet: The prophets are men and women who, caught
up in the whirlwind of the Word of God, allow it to become
so much part of them that when they speak God's
Word, not their own, they speak the message and values
of Jesus.

Stance: It depends on where you stand as to what you see:
but the baptised are called to take a dynamic stand on the
journey of faith, on the continuing climb of the holy
mountain, or on the pilgrimage through the desert on their
exodus of freedom.

Resistance: Having taken the mystical-prophetic stance,
Paul Ricoeur[9] says we need to adopt the hermeneutics of
suspicion. Hermeneutics is that area of philosophy that
helps us interpret not only texts (e.g. the Word of God),
but also our own experience and reality. Thus, we baptised
need to resist prophetically the many competitors for our
allegiance; for example, flirtations with fundamentalists, of
all kinds whether they be religious, social or political
fundamentalists; we need to treat with suspicion the easy
answers of the neo-conservatives, whether they be inside
or outside our church.

Hope: In spite of the mess things seem to be in, we have
to be men and women with a hope in the future. We have
to believe that in spite of the possibilities of evil brought
about by the human heart, we can be people full of hope

9   David Stewart, The Hermeneutics of Suspicion, in *The Journal of
Literature and Theology* 3, 1989, pp. 296-307.

because we are full of the Spirit of God and the human
spirit. This reminds me of the denouement of Umberto
Eco's, *The Name of the Rose*. Eco has William of Basker-
ville say to the murderous Jorge that the devil is not the
prince of matter, but arrogance of the spirit, faith without
a smile, truth that is never seized by doubt. He is grim
because he knows where he is going, and, in moving, he
always returns from whence he came.[10]

3. RESURGENCE OF INTEREST IN THE MYSTICS

Given the renewal of the understanding of the universal
call to holiness of all the baptised, the meditations of theologians who say that all Christians are called to be contemplatives (Karl Rahner, Gustavo Gutierrez, Segundo Galilea
and David Tracy, to name but a few), there has been a great
resurgence of interest in the mystics of our tradition. Allied
to this is the interest of liberation theologians to present
a spirit of liberation, and many have rediscovered the
mystics, especially one of the Carmelite tradition, St John
of the Cross − whom they see as a mystic who can lead
men and women of today to an inner liberation.

St John of the Cross the poet[11]

The key to understanding St John's contribution to
Christian spirituality is to see him as a sublime poet.

10   Umberto Eco, *The Name of the Rose*. Picador, London, 1984, p.477.
11   St John was born in Spain in 1542. He became a Carmelite friar and
     joined St Teresa of Avila in the reform of the Carmelite order. He
     died in 1591, was canonised in 1726 and declared a doctor of the
     universal Church by Pope Pius XI in 1926. St John of the Cross' feast
     day is December 14.

Evelyn Woodward[12] has noted that the poet lives with a sensitivity which is open to the nuances of life and the vagaries of the human spirit. Poets share their perceptions and heightened awareness in language and metaphor. They hear, see and speak in ways many of us cannot. They are the ones who contemplate rather than do, they see value rather than utility, they evoke rather than analyse, they point rather than grasp, they dream rather than plan.

The moods of poets illuminate what many see only dimly; they strip away our illusions, masks and pretensions, leaving us exposed and vulnerable. Poetry arises from contemplation and silence. T.S. Eliot says that poets are alone and often prone to suffering brought about by their supersensitivity. Poets see beyond themselves, but are aware of their own inner life and experience, and so empathise and generalise from it.

> *O guiding night!*
> *O Night more lovely than the dawn,*
> *O Night that has united*
> *The lover with His beloved,*
> *Transforming the beloved in her Lover.*
>
> *Upon my flowering breast*
> *Which I kept wholly for Him alone,*
> *There he lay sleeping,*
> *And I caressing Him*
> *There is a breeze from the fanning Cedars.*
>
> The Dark Night[13]

As poet, mystic and contemplative the soul of St John of the Cross leapt into rapturous heights. He found it

---

12 Evelyn Woodward, *Poets, Prophets and Pragmatists*. CollinsDove, Blackburn, Victoria, 1987, pp. 12-16.
13 Translation: A. Peers as quoted in R. Sencourt, *Carmelite and Poet*. Hollis and Carter, London, 1943, p. 120.

difficult to use ordinary language to describe his relationship to God and often used the analogy of bride and bridegroom. His imagination used the colours and patterns of symbolic language even to the point where he confessed that he scarcely knew what he was saying. Poems like his cannot be analysed simply in a rational way, but listened to as one listens to a melody of Mozart. His poems have a strange dreamlike quality, like a metaphysical fire — a kind of white heat which touches our very souls.

One dark night
Fired with love's urgent longings
— Ah, the sheer grace —
I went out unseen,
My house being now all stilled.[14]

In his poetry there is an abandonment to love, based on the spiritual longing and desire to be united with God. His poetry is fully human, earthy and at times simply erotic love poetry.

Thomas Merton says the poet is an innocent with no magic of words 'only life in all its unpredictability and all its freedom'.[15] Thus, the freedom of the poet is to remain outside the temporal imprisonment of institutional living and to span past, present and future, bringing to light what is best in history to bear on the struggles in the present and pointing to the unknown future with hope and love.

St John, the poet, being a person of discernment, was sensitive to the injustices and exaggerations of his time, and in his innocence he made people aware of them. Poets are

---

14 Translation: K. Kavanaugh OCD and O. Rodriguez OCD, *The Collected Works of Saint John of the Cross* ICS Publications, Washington DC, 1979, p. 711.
15 Thomas Merton, *Raids on the Unspeakable*, New Directions, New York, 1966, p. 159.

uncomfortable people with whom to be. Certainly, toward the end of his life those with power did not want him close to them. He called on his fellow religious to examine stagnation in their lives and institutions — he did this by force of the sanctity of his life and the power of his poetry. He was a silent contemplative who suffered, not only because of his own empathy, but because he threatened the powerful. Out of his silence he caressed and challenged all who read his poetry.

Liberation

Among the elements of contemporary theology, the theology of liberation seems to dialogue well with the Carmelite tradition and, in particular, the spirituality of St John of the Cross. Much of the writing of St John of the Cross is to show us how to free ourselves from the tyranny of the ego.[16] When we keep looking at Jesus, we make our choices in line with the values of Jesus. He continually calls us to transcend ourselves and keep reaching for the Father, by a denial of our self-sufficiency that comes from the prompting of our ego.

The power of our ego leads us to make ourselves the centre of our own universe. While we all have basic human rights to protect and promote, there is a danger that we will be overwhelmed by a selfish notion of our own self-importance. St John of the Cross says that if we want to love God, if we want to begin to ascend the mountain, we must choose against our own self-importance. We have to take

---

16 R. Burrows, *Ascent to Love*, Dimension Books, Denville, NJ, 1987, pp. 37-48.

ourselves out of the spotlight, and see ourselves as members of a community we are meant to serve. The sincere follower of Jesus must wish to become the servant of all and not the centre of attention. The drive of the ego often brings an enslavement to human respect where we are ruled by what others think of us. St John of the Cross says that we must be freed from this slavery if we want to love God in contemplation. As a servant of all, or thinking little of ourselves, we are not likely to be interested in the frailties of our neighbour and thus be a sort of person who will sit in judgment on others. In his writings St John of the Cross says that when we free ourselves from the tyranny of the ego, the slavery of self-importance, we begin to experience the refreshment of the Holy Spirit. This comes in the form of the infused theological virtues of faith, hope and love which help us to make right judgments, because a person overcome by selfishness cannot make the correct decisions.

The contribution of St John of the Cross to Christian tradition offers a spirituality of substance, a spirituality of personal and interior liberation. This requires primarily a commitment to Jesus, his person and his message that can give men and women the only true liberation. The gospel of Jesus calls men and women to use gospel values to create a new heaven, a new earth, and so become the new creation. To liberate, we must be liberated. This means that we must be concerned continually about being free from our own inner idols before we can free people of injustices and poverty. Without a parallel concern for inner conversion, our efforts at social liberation will be in jeopardy.

To be free from our false gods

Today the theological discussion also raises the God

question. What kind of God do we follow? Who is the
authentic God of revelation? Who is the Father of Jesus
of the gospels – the Jesus to whom we have committed
ourselves?

This is a matter for our personal and inner liberation –
we need to abandon any imperfect notion of God and
convert ourselves to the one, true God – the one who
cannot be manipulated, nor domesticated, nor allow us to
remain comfortable and cosy. We are called to the God who
challenges us to conversion, flexibility and creativity, the
God of mercy, justice and solidarity. Only if we believe in
and follow this God will our spirituality develop our
commitment to the peace and justice in the world. St John
of the Cross is someone in our tradition who liberates God.
He teaches us to let God be God, and allow God to mould
us according to his Spirit. Since there can be no liberation
without our liberating ourselves from false notions of God,
the Carmelite tradition has much to say to liberation
theology in the spirit of humble dialogue.

St John's Dark Night is the itinerary that helps us find
God without deforming him. According to St John's
spiritual synthesis, we liberate God from our imperfect
ways of believing in and loving our God. One of the
difficulties of understanding St John of the Cross today
stems from his poetic language. One concept which may
help translate him to the contemporary church is the
notion of our inner liberation from false notions of God.
This will lead us to a clearer understanding of his symbols
of night and nothingness. We can also take his notions of
solitude, desert and retreat and adapt them to modern
spirituality that sees the need for quiet reflections, alone
with God. The desert is a form of liberation, as St Thérèse
understood, because it forces us to face the truth about
ourselves, our lives and our relationships. In the desert and

retreat we are stripped of all our illusions about ourselves
– we are set free.

To love with total humanity

The gift of the sanjuanist teaching is that the key to life
is love, and we should love God and humans with the love
of a person fully human. This means we love with our
head and our heart, our spirit and our body, our intellect
and will and our feelings, emotions, and desires. St John
of the Cross reminds us also if we love as a person fully
alive it will bring suffering – a word he uses frequently
in his love poetry: 'wounding'. It does not mean that we
sadistically seek suffering and morbidity, but he shows that
the very experience of love brings with it a certain amount
of suffering and hurt. St John of the Cross opens this up
for us as he reaches high peaks in his mystical poetry –
his spirit sings of the transforming love which God gives
him, and which he describes with earthy passion, like a
love affair, or like a marriage or like a tough climb up the
mountain of Carmel.

Liberation for Australians

More particularly and closer to home, there may be areas
where Australians need to seek liberation. Matthew Fox has
suggested that people in the so-called first world countries,
or in overdeveloped societies, need liberation from many
addictions.[17] He quotes Anne Wilson Schaef who defines

17 Matthew Fox, Addiction in Overdeveloped Cultures, in *Creation
    Spirituality*, Jan/Feb 1991, pp. 28, 29, 52.

addiction as any process over which we are powerless, taking control of us, causing us to do and think things that are inconsistent with our personal values and leading us to become progressively more compulsive and obsessive.[18] Fox believes that we begin our liberation from addictions by starting with joy, a gift of the Holy Spirit. A dimension of the addictive personality is co-dependency, which is characterised by feelings of low self-worth, being a workaholic, wanting always to be liked and being a public longsufferer.

We can help people to liberate themselves by encouraging interdependence. This attacks the issue of low self-esteem by teaching people that we are created in the image and likeness of God by whom we are originally blessed. We get on with liberating ourselves from addictions by letting go of our self-importance, knowing ourselves honestly and rejecting denial, learning from our mistakes and rejecting perfectionism, joyfully co-operating with God and our companion sojourners to make the best of the world that God has given us.

Another area for liberation for Australians is the concern for our Aboriginal brothers and sisters. We need to work co-operatively with the original Australians to liberate them from the many injustices from which they suffer: inadequacies in their rights to land, adequate and appropriate housing, education and health care; lack of justice from law enforcement agencies, from the courts, from government bureaucracies; feelings of alienation from mainstream Australian society, churches and private charities.

There need to be more efforts on the part of the Church in Australia to heal hurts of the past, to bring about

18 *Ibid.*, p.28.

reconciliation between Aborigines and Catholics, between Aborigines and white Australians. In this way maybe white Australians will be liberated from what Manning Clark calls 'our original sin'.

A future spirituality

Through a renewed appreciation of the great mystics of the past we can name our present and have some power over shaping our future. Our concerns for a richer spiritual life will help us answer the call of the Church to a universal holiness, or a mysticism for everyone in everyday life. A future spirituality will be characterised by a more passionate seeking after God, deeper relationships between people, and an attempt to integrate the ordinary aspects of our daily lives with ecumenism, science and technology, humanism, the environment and an on-going transformation.

Gregory Burke OCD

THE LIFE AND TIMES OF ST JOHN OF THE CROSS

Spain in the sixteenth century was not a European holiday destination. Under Charles V it had become the predominant European power. His son, Phillip II, king from 1556-98, expanded that power. Outside Spain itself, he ruled what is now Belgium, Holland and Luxembourg, Sardinia, Sicily, the Kingdom of Naples, as well as the Duchy of Milan, and the traditional Hapsburg dominions in Austria. For the English, the Dutch, and even the Pope, who was an Italian, it was too much. Spain was a menacing empire, with a huge and successful army. That army was to be victorious until the rout of the Spanish Armada in 1588. Moreover, Spain was not a purely European power. After Columbus in 1492 it had control of the greater part of the Americas and was intensely exploiting them for its own benefit. The year 1492 was eventful: Granada, the final Islamic stronghold in Spain, was defeated.

With that victory the long centuries of the Reconquest
were complete. In their pride of victory the Catholic
monarchs decided to expel all the Jews from Spain. The
Jews were given a choice: either convert to Catholicism or
go into exile. There grew an obsession with racial purity
and orthodox faith. It was feared that Jews had converted
from expediency and were not sincere believers. As
Catholicism was the unifying political ideology as well as
a personal faith this called for drastic measures. The
Spanish Inquisition was a means of state control. Those
born of *conversos* stock invited the particular scrutiny of the
Inquisition.

Early years

In 1542, John of the Cross was born of such *conversos* stock.
His father Gonzalo de Yepes came from a wealthy family.
After losing both his parents he was brought up by his
uncles in Toledo. They were prosperous silk merchants.
Others of the family were eminent ecclesiastics. Gonzalo
seemed to have an assured future until, on business for his
uncles, he met Catalina Alvarez, a poor weaver, and fell in
love with her. On their marriage he was cut off by his
family who refused to have anything to do with him again.
The price of Gonzalo's love was his fall from a mansion
in beautiful Toledo at the top of the cloth trade to the sweat
shop in dusty Fontiveros at the bottom. To support his
family he joined Catalina as a weaver. The family's poverty
was real.

There were born to Gonzalo and Catalina three sons.
John was the youngest. Sometime after John's birth
Gonzalo died. Catalina was left destitute and refused help
by her wealthy in-laws. After the second son, Luis, also

died she moved to Medina del Campo where Francisco, the eldest, worked to support the family.

Catalina was a woman of extraordinary character who in her poverty cared for abandoned infants, had them baptised and arranged for adoptions. John had to be placed in an orphanage, the Collegio de la Doctrina, where he learnt to read and write and was prepared for a trade. He was a spectacularly unsuccessful apprentice, being sacked by all the tradesmen. Instead he found employment in a convent sacristy where he won favour by his quiet piety.

He began work at the Hospital de las Bubas, where advanced cases of syphilis were treated, and he nursed the sixteenth century equivalent of AIDS sufferers. His ability was noticed by the hospital administrator, who arranged that he be enrolled at the new Jesuit School as a part-time student. To be a priest was the obvious career for a poor but studious youth. He was offered a chaplaincy at the hospital, if he were to be ordained.

But John's heart was elsewhere. At the age of 21 he entered the Carmelite Priory of Santa Ana in Medina. A year later he was professed as Brother John of St Matthias. In the same year, 1564, he entered the University of Salamanca to study arts. He completed the course in three years and was ordained a priest. He returned to Medina to say his first Mass with his mother.

But John was not a happy man. He was fervent and disillusioned at the failure of his brethren to take the religious life as seriously as he did. Understandably, with this attitude, he was not a popular fellow in the Carmelite Priory in Salamanca. John wanted to leave the Carmelites and join an order that took silence and solitude more seriously: the Carthusians.

Teresa of Avila

This journey home to Medina in September 1567 was to
be a major turning point for John. But not in the way he
had imagined. There he met Mother Teresa, come from
Avila to found a new monastery of her nuns. Teresa was
delighted when she met John. She persuaded him not to
join the Carthusians but her group of reformed Carmelites.
She wanted to begin a group of men who would accompany
the sisters on the spiritual journey, share the same style of
life while being available for mission. John agreed, with the
proviso he did not have to wait long.

Teresa had founded St Joseph's in Avila five years earlier.
She wanted a smaller, friendlier, poorer, more united and
prayerful community than was possible in the vast Incarnation convent where she had been a Carmelite nun.

She sought to renew the church by strengthening it from
within. It was a time of crisis, the Reformation was spread-
ing daily, churches were being destroyed, the Eucharist was
being profaned, souls were being lost. The world was in
flames. She thought that since the Lord had so few friends
those he had should be good ones. She was part of a loose
alliance of religious reformers including John of Avila, the
Jesuits, certain charismatic lay women like Mari Diaz in
Avila and the Discalced Franciscan Peter of Alcantara.
What united the new movements were the ideals of
apostolic service and concern for the church, the focus of
interiority rather than externals, mental prayer, religious
autonomy and freedom from aristocratic patrons, simplicity and poverty. Teresa brought these features to the
context of a contemplative community of women.

Teresa had permission from the Carmelite General to
found two monasteries of 'contemplative Carmelites' within
the friars' province of Castile. The limitations of this brief,

the different perspectives of Teresa, the king, and the Carmelite General provided the materials for the drama that later was to envelop John. Not knowing the future, he went back to Salamanca to study theology for a year. That was the extent of his formal theological education. In August 1568 he joined Teresa in Valladolid where she was making another foundation. There he observed the life of the sisters at firsthand: 'both the mortifications practised, the form of sisterly affection and the recreations, which are all followed with such moderation' as Teresa wrote in her Foundations. She goes on in her usual ironical tone, 'He was so good a man that I, at least, could have learned more from him than he from me. I did not do so however, but merely showed him the way the sisters live'.

In November 1568, at the age of 26, John took off his shoes and put on the rough habit Teresa had sewn for him. Anthony of Jesus who considered himself the first Discalced friar, was put out by their one-upmanship. With a couple of companions they began the life of the first male Discalced Carmelites at the tiny remote hamlet of Duruelo, where they renewed their profession according to the Carmelite Rule. John, as a sign of the new beginning, changed his name to John of the Cross. Life in Duruelo was primitive; the community was fervent in prayer and enthusiasic about taking the gospel to the uncatechised locals.

Troubled times

As the new movement grew it suffered from a lack of clear leadership, identity and unity, still being a couple of houses within the province of Castile. A crisis became apparent at the second house in Pastrana. It had been founded by ex-hermits whose bizarre penances and other eccentricities substituted for formation for those who joined. John went there in 1572 to sort things out. In September of the same year he was asked to support Teresa who had been elected Prioress of the Incarnation against her own better judgment and the wishes of many of the members. John was the confessor to the nuns. Here he showed the quality of his spiritual direction and he remained on even after Teresa left in July 1573. While John's relationship with Teresa deepened to their mutual benefit, he was effectively sidelined as far from leadership of the friars.

In Spain there was a dual jurisdiction for religious. While a good Catholic, Phillip II was more in control of the Spanish Church than Rome. He was deeply involved in efforts to reform the religious orders. To this end he obtained apostolic visitators. Those for the Carmelites were two Dominicans who possessed more authority over the Spanish Carmelites than their own General. Difficulties increased when one of the visitators, Vargas, delegated his faculties to a young Discalced friar, Jerome Gracian, in 1573. He received even wider faculties the next year from Ormaneto, the Apostolic Nuncio. In this peculiar situation Gracian gave his brethren permission for new foundations and attempted to reform the friars of the Observance. It was not a happy or lasting solution.

Bad communication and uncertainty on both sides about the exact nature of Gracian's faculties made for growing tension. The Carmelite General Chapter meeting at Piacenza in 1575 adopted stern measures to curtail the new movement which seemed to be out of their control. John was arrested and imprisoned in the Carmelite Priory at Medina for a short time in 1576. He then returned to his post as the confessor to the Incarnation. In June 1577 the Nuncio died and was succeeded by Sega who was hostile to the new movement.

The storm broke. On December 2 or 3, 1577, John was kidnapped and taken hostage by Carmelites of the Observance. In freezing cold, on terrible back roads over the Guadarrama mountains, John was spirited to Toledo where he was held prisoner in a tiny, airless cell at the Carmelite Priory. He was accused of being a rebel against the properly constituted authority of the Order. He was abused and maltreated but remained resolute in his adherence to the reform. Teresa was beside herself with anxiety at his eerie disappearance. His brethren were more phlegmatic.

John's dark night

For John himself this was not just a physical and emotional trial but a spiritual one as well. His dark night he experienced as the cruelty of God. But in this extremity his faith was purified and his sense of himself re-made. His dependence on God was absolute. There was no one and nothing else that could possibly help. So the darkness of prison did not have the defining word. There was also the burning truth and saving beauty of the love of God. From this experience John created his poems. In the end it was for him a privileged time of grace. He had been given a share in the cross of Christ and experienced its liberating power.

As the months dragged on and it became clear that John would not be intimidated or broken, he became a burden to his captors. In time he was given a new gaoler who was sympathetic, who allowed him paper and pen so the poems were written down. He was also allowed to get some exercise in a corridor. John decided to take advantage of the situation and escape. This he did just after the feast of the

Assumption, 1578, by breaking out of the cell whose lock he had loosened surreptitiously. Using his cut-up blanket as a rope he scaled down the wall of the priory hoping to find a tiny ledge to prevent his falling down the cliffs over the Tagus River. After this desperate adventure he made his way to the Discalced Carmelite nuns and thence hiding and safety.

To Andalusia

The Discalced friars had not accepted their excommunication, so in October they called an illegal chaper which John attended. They appealed to Rome and elected their own provincial. John went as prior to a small monastery in rural Andalusia called El Calvario.

Nearby were the nuns at Beas where Anne of Jesus was prioress. John told his story and recited his poems. The curiosity of the nuns soon turned to admiration and a desire for guidance from John. So John went each weekend to be with the sisters, to hear their confessions, give conferences and explain his spiritual doctrine. From this relationship there grew the great commentaries on the poems: *The Ascent of Mount Carmel* and *The Spiritual Canticle*.

John spent ten years in Andalusia. At first he found the change difficult – his worse complaint was being away from the saints of his native Castile: Teresa, and his mother and brother, Francisco, to whom he was very close. John's time in Andalusia was very fruitful: he found houses of sisters and friars, he wrote major works, he became Vicar provincial and travelled almost continuously throughout the south. It has been estimated he travelled over 16 000 miles during his life. As well, he was close to people who valued him as a friend and spiritual guide, not least Mother Anne of Jesus and Ana de Penalosa.

In 1581 the Discalced received a measure of their longed-for independence and recognition. John attended the chapter of that year and later met Teresa again for the last time. His mother had died the previous year during the great flu epidemic.

Leadership

In 1588 John attended the first general Chapter of the Discalced in Madrid and was elected first definitor. Shortly after, he went to Segovia as prior. This was a new foundation in an old Trinitarian monastery made possible by a donation of his friend Ana de Penalosa. John's idea of the dignity of his office was the same here as it was in Granada where he had also been prior.

He liked nothing better than to be working with his hands in the garden or on building sites with the labourers. His habit was therefore scruffy and he always wanted to be seen as the least important of the brethren. His old skills as a nurse also came to the fore whenever any of the brethren were sick. His kindness and generosity was proverbial. He also liked to pray in the beauty of creation. To that end he bought a field behind the monastery where he could go and pray in a little cave in the cliff. The cave may have been small but the view was breathtaking, and still is.

While in Segovia John had a vision of Christ who asked him what reward he would like for all he had done. John in the midst of these happy years asked not for power and recognition but the cross so that he might be more like his Lord. He asked 'to suffer and to be looked down upon'. He warned his brother not to be surprised at the trials that were soon to come to him.

John had had an important role in the leadership team of the Discalced Carmelites but the new leader was a man of very different character. Nicholas Doria was a banker who decided to introduce efficiency and organisational control and so he stressed authority, strict observance, severely limiting the apostolate especially mission work and the intellectual life. In doing this he had raised opposition from the nuns led by Anne of Jesus, now prioress in Madrid, and among the friars by Jerome Gracian, the great friend of Teresa and Doria's predecessor. He was furious and ruthlessly attempted to crush them. John could not remain silent as he saw the ambition behind the new policies of his henchmen. He spoke the truth and suffered the consequences. At the chapter of 1591, as he had predicted, he was not elected to any office and a vendetta was launched against him. Because of John's moral authority it was not enough to remove him from office; he had to be discredited or even exiled to Mexico. This shameful persecution raised very serious questions about the spirit of the new movement.

Exile and death

John was sent out of the way to an isolated little monastery called la Penuela, in Andalusia. Spiritually he was, as ever, a free man and not a victim. As he said at the time, 'Where there is no love put love and you will find love'. John was in La Penuela only a few months when he became sick and it was decided to send him to another house for medical treatment. He asked to go to Ubeda because he was not well known there. He was disgracefully treated by the prior. When Anthony of Jesus, his companion from the heroic days of Duruelo but now provincial in Andalusia, heard he was sick he rushed to his side. Anthony insisted everything be done that could help the sick man. Even those who had resented his presence were won over by John's thoughtfulness, gentleness and patience.

As he lay dying the brethren began the *de Profundis* and other said prayers. John asked instead for some passages from the *Song of Songs*, the passionate love poetry of the Old Testament. 'What marvellous pearls, what marvellous pearls,' he said. When the bell rang for Matins he asked what it was. When told he said, 'Glory to God. I shall say them in heaven'.

Moments later he died. It was December 14, 1591. John was 49. He died as he lived; his spirit was victorious in suffering; his holiness was obvious to the people of the town, and, at last, to his own brethren.

Brian Pitman O.Carm.

HOW TO READ THE WORKS OF ST JOHN OF THE CROSS

Without succumbing to all the excesses and trivialities and narcissism with which New Age phenomena barrage us, it is indisputable that the New Age's interest in the mystical — very often simplistically defined — is an instance of a spirit of the times needing to be transformed into a sign of the times. There we will find a cultural call to a return to the great mystical tradition of world religions, of Christianity and of the Catholic Church. For that reason, familiarity with St John of the Cross' writings — which are probably the most respected writings ecumenically and on the inter-faith scene of all Christian mystical writings — becomes extremely relevant to the future of Christianity, religions and our world.[1]

---

1   For a popular presentation of this theme: cf. G.A. Maloney SJ, *Mysticism and the New Age*, Alba, New York, 1991.

Doubts about mysticism

Looking back to a first phase of my association with St John of the Cross I resonate – as thousands of people can – with an autobiographical comment of the contemporary Jesuit spiritual writer, Thomas H. Green, who wrote that during the early years of his Jesuit formation the writings of St John of the Cross were kept in a locked section of the library, 'because they were considered *mystical* in a way that was un-Jesuit'.[2]

Un-Jesuit may refer to a distinction sometimes made between Ignatian mysticism as kataphatic (of light) and Sanjuanist mysticism as apophatic (of darkness). But not only Jesuits restricted the reading of the writings of St John of the Cross and other mystics. Everywhere during the early twentieth century, both Catholic and Protestant theology showed extreme caution about mystical experience. Three factors from the prevailing culture and life of the Church at the time contributed to this anti-mystical thrust.

First was the Catholic reaction, through the Council of Trent, to the doctrine of 'good works' as it was understood to have been eschewed by the Protestant reformers. Any diminishment of active cooperation in our salvation, such as seemed to be inherent in a defence of the growth in passivity as part of a mystical experience, was regarded with suspicion in Catholic teaching.

Teresa of Avila encountered this suspicion of her writings because of the presence of the heresy Illuminism which was rife in the Spain of her times. But, in regard to the works of St John of the Cross, this was not the issue. The

2   Thomas H. Green, *Spiritual Life* 17, 1991, pp. 67-76; cf. p. 67.

problem arose several decades later, not in Spain but in France and the Netherlands, and was (and is) about the commentaries that had been written on the writings of St John of the Cross.

Quietism

This time the interfering heresy was called Quietism. This caused an extraordinary paralysing fear of the mystical in the Church. The study has yet to be made of how this fear truncated spiritual life, particularly in France and the Lowlands, but also in the rest of Europe; and through the missionary activity of Europeans, to most parts of the world. The result was twofold.

First, the reading of mystical writings was not encouraged, and many writers were put on the Index of Prohibited Books. Second, where commentaries on mystical writings were produced, they tended to reflect the concern in those days to safeguard, in what today may be considered an exaggerated way, an orthodox understanding of the doctrine of 'good works'. This meant an emphasis on the ascetical rather than the mystical aspect of his teaching. And it is the commentaries on John's writings, rather than the writings themselves, about which contemporary study has reservations.

Ascetical and mystical

The difficulties about these commentaries is enshrined in a distinction which, without the era of Quietism and its companion Jansenism, made the ascetical and the mystical

two distinct paths to God. So much of what has been
written by way of commentary on St John of the Cross'
works, and presentation of his personality, has been from
an ascetical viewpoint. It was the era, first of what Louis
Buoyer has called 'dolorism', and later of 19th century
'pietism'.

Both movements disfigured the teaching and personality
of St John of the Cross. Almost from the beginning of
commentaries on his writings, the emphasis has been on
the ascetical activity of the human person as part of the
'good works' by which one cooperates with grace in working out our salvation.

The distinction between the ascetical and the mystical
was viewed in some circles as the way to holiness of the
many (the ascetical) and the way of the few (the mystical).
By others it was proposed that the ascetical was the way
into the mystical. Only in our own times is it being realised
that the mystical is the way to the ascetical. God's love
(which is the nature of the mystical) moves us to the
ascetical task of opening ourselves to the action of the
Spirit who conforms our humanity to the humanity of
Christ, and to the image of God.

St John of the Cross' writings

A second phase in my acquaintance with the works of St
John of the Cross was when – as in the case of Fr Green
– I was allowed to read this great Carmelite mystic during
my theological studies. I faltered again, not being able to
persevere much beyond *The Ascent of Mount Carmel* and
a very desultory reading of *The Dark Night of the Soul*. And
that, by any standard, was quite an achievement. I find, in

recent years, that even in this scenario, which many others also share, we walk in eminent company.

It is recorded that Cardinal Newman, after he received a gift copy of the first translation into English, made in 1864 by David Lewis, evidently did not proceed beyond the opening pages; the Introduction by Cardinal Wiseman, and the first two chapters of *The Ascent of Mount Carmel* were the only pages that had been cut.[3] It seems that he, more a lover of patristic spirituality, never read all the works of the saint, and perhaps never proceeded beyond those opening chapters of *The Ascent of Mount Carmel*.

This led me to ponder whether the order or arrangement of the works was perhaps the stumbling block. It dates, I believe, from about 1630 and was first made by Fray Jeronimo de San Jose, an earlier biographer of John. Editions of the collected works usually present first *The Ascent of Mount Carmel*, second *The Dark Night of the Soul*, then *The Spiritul Canticle* and last *The Living Flame of Love*. That order represents the logical development of a transformation of the human to the divine. But does it represent the theological reality of a life directed by the fact that God has first loved us (1 Jn 4:10)?

The recovery of this truth, largely ignored in several centuries of a rationalist methodology, is basic to a contemporary pursuit of a paradigm change in theology. In this new paradigm the mystical experience is seen as crucial to theology in the strict sense of that word, namely, as faith seeking understanding.

3   cf. Phillip Boyce ODC, The Writings of John of the Cross in Britain and Ireland, *Teresianum*, 1991, pp. 97-121.

God has first loved us

My third attempt to familiarise myself with the writings
of St John of the Cross was about fifteen years ago, towards
the end of my seminary teaching career. Even though I had
nursed a conviction that the order in which the various
works of St John of the Cross was the reason so many
people did not persevere through his various works, it was
not until it was very obvious that the new paradigm for
theology is inextricably linked to mystical experience, that
I turned anew to the writings of the one who, if not for
the Church as a whole, at least for my Carmelite tradition,
is an expositor of the ineffable experience of divine love in
the human heart. But as I read and reflect the more, I am
aware that both the sacred and the secular sciences are
listening to the mystical experience of the past, and looking
for the mystical experience as the source of authentic
knowledge.

Mindful of the emphasis on experience I began this third
study by reading the poetry of St John of the Cross, in
which I was particularly captured by the extraordinary
Christology they contain. Secondly, and most importantly,
I read John's writing with the awareness that God has first
loved me, and continues to love me unconditionally. Thirdly, I read with an awareness of the unity of the spiritual
life that began with baptism and continues throughout life
and glory. In all this I found myself sustained by a point
of commentary John makes, on *The Spiritual Canticle* 2,8.
Of the verse 'Tell Him that I sicken, suffer and die' John
writes:

> *It should be pointed out that in this verse the soul does no*
> *more than disclose her need and suffering to the Beloved.*
> *The discreet lover does not care to ask for what she lacks*
> *and desires, but only indicates this need that the Beloved*

may do what He pleases --- There are three reasons for this: first, the Lord knows what is suitable for us better than we do; second, the Beloved has more compassion when He beholds the needs and resignation of a soul that loves Him; third, the soul is better safeguarded against self-love and possessiveness by indicating its lack, rather than asking for what in its opinion is wanting.[4]

A journey and an encounter

The result of this third attempt to read St John of the Cross is that for me *The Spiritual Canticle* and *The Living Flame* are what I would describe as maps of the way in which the Lord lavishes his love. *The Ascent* and *The Dark Night* are keen insights into what the way of faith and hope and love will mean for our human nature.

From a different point of view, a recent study has described the differences between what are really two genres of writing by the Carmelite mystic:

The Ascent of Mount Carmel *and* The Dark Night of the Soul *represent a journey and a process of purification which help us to encounter God without deforming him, but rather letting him be God in us:* The Spiritual Canticle *and* The Living Flame *represent the encounter and the experience of love with a God who has been set free from our projections, manipulations and enslavement, a God who makes us share in his way of being.*[5]

---

4   Kavanaugh and Rodriguez, eds, p. 427.
5   *Walking Side by Side with all Men and Women*, Institutum Carmelitanum, Rome, 1991, pp. 56-57.

The order of reading of St John of the Cross

The latter observation need not take away from the now more widely accepted view that one should first read the commentaries on *The Spiritual Canticle* and *The Living Flame*. But, considering all the works of St John of the Cross, I would propose the following order in which they should be read:

- all the poetical works
- the letters
- the prologues (in this order) to: *The Living Flame of Love*, *The Spiritual Canticle*, *The Ascent of Mount Carmel*, *The Dark Night of the Soul*
- the commentaries on *The Living Flame*, *The Spiritual Canticle*
- other writings, which, along with the letters, are published as the 'minor works'
- Book I, chapter 14, of *The Ascent of Mount Carmel*
- the commentaries on *The Ascent of Mount Carmel* and *The Dark Night of the Soul*.

Why this order?

Central to this suggestion is that we begin with *The Living Flame of Love* or at least *The Spiritual Canticle*. Putting *The Living Flame* first is, I admit, arbitrary, and is based on *The Living Flame*'s brevity, and on the exalted destiny it shows God to have for us. Begin with the briefer, and more exalted description of what God wants to do for us. The crucial point is that the commentary on either *The Living Flame* or *The Spiritual Canticle* is the entry to our appreciation of the writings of St John of the Cross as an appreciation of what John knows from his own experience

God has in store for those in whom the gift of his love grows.

The point at issue is that a theology of the spiritual life attends to what God is doing, and where his 'first loving us' wants to lead us. This is not precisely a revolutionary viewpoint in contemporary theology so much as a recovery of how God's revelation of himself is of the primacy of his initiative in our experience of growing into Christ.

Then, too, we need to recognise that poetry, rather than prose, is John's *métier*. In fact, his prose is, for the most part, associated with three poems and his commentary on them. Yet, while we do not neglect the remainder of his poetry, we also do not ignore the intense theological acumen contained in his clumsy prose and its highly technical language of what is called Scholasticism.

The Letters, as one author suggests, are a valuable introduction to the personality of John, which until very recent times has been appraised within a maelstrom of conflicting historical details about John's experiences as a Carmelite, and by hagiographical tendencies to fit a subject into prevailing but false views of holiness.

Compulsory reading

The final place given to what John intended to be *The Dark Night of the Ascent of Mount Carmel* is not to belittle these two great commentaries. It is rather that they are such complex works, both unfinished, and about which there are still many unresolved problems. But they are both necessary reading. Be attentive especially to *The Ascent of Mount Carmel* (Bk 1:13,11) which relates to the diagram of the mountain. Note, too, the extraordinary keenness of mind in *The Dark Night* (Bk 1:27) about imperfection associated with a spiritual view of the seven deadly sins. These will make us keenly aware that even our practice of religion can be bedevilled by human imperfections that hinder the surrender to God.

It has recently been suggested that John's minute examination of human behaviour is really applying in a good cause, and in an impersonal way, a tendency he had as a young friar to be something of a nitpicker about the faulty behaviour of his peers.

Returning to the list of the order in which to read the works of our author: the suggestion about Book 1:14 (especially paragraph two) is borrowed from an article by Thomas Moore OCD.[6] The core of paragraph two seems to be that the love of one's Spouse is not the only requisite for conquering the strength of the sensitive appetites; an enkindling with longings of love is also necessary.

These words are a comment on the second verse: 'Fired with love's urgent longings' – of the poem named for its first verse 'One dark night'. Unfortunately, in the next paragraph (14:3) John goes on to say this is not the place for a discussion of how easy, sweet and delightful these longings for their Spouse make all the trials and dangers of this night seem. It is better to experience all of this and meditate upon it than to write of it.

Interestingly, the comment illustrates a problem about *The Ascent*. As a commentary on a poem which begins 'One dark night' John is obliged first to explain how this night is caused by a purgation of the appetites; and four times he comes back to begin to explain this opening verse. This seems to give an unusual priority to the 'night', at

6   Carmelite Digest, 6, 1991, 57-64.

least in comparison to the much briefer commentary he gives, three times, on the second verse: 'Fired with love's urgent longings'. But, *The Spiritual Canticle* and *The Living Flame* are, in a sense, also commentary on that verse.

How do we read St John of the Cross?

Beyond the suggestion that we approach the writings of St John of the Cross from a mystical rather than an ascetical viewpoint, and that we follow a progression in reading his writings that is different from the way in which they are presented in editions of his *Collected Works*, let us address other aspects of the question: How do we read texts of the Carmelite mystic?

A prime answer is that they should be read in the spirit of what Christian tradition calls 'Lectio divina' (literally, 'divine reading' or reading done with the eyes of the Holy Spirit). This is a methodology that is seen as of prime importance in discovering the relevance for today of recorded divine revelation.

To help with this pursuit of the practice of 'Lectio divina' I refer to an article in *Carmelite* 9.[7] It is authored by Carlos Mesters, O.Carm. and is entitled 'Meditating Day and Night on the Law of the Lord and Keeping Vigil in Prayer'. Though the article is subtitled 'Reflections on the Prayerful Reading of the Bible', the article also applies *pari passu* to works which belong to what we call the unwritten word of God preserved in the monuments of the life of the Church. In that spirit, a letter from the Council of the

7   *Carmelite* 9, 1991, No 5. pp. 8-11.

Carmelite Order to its members[8] recommends that 'the writings of John of the Cross could be read in their entirety as a "lectio divina"' (cf. 1 *Ascent* 22; *Flame* 3:34).

If you read John's prologue to his various major works you will see that he uses terms such as the need of recollection and similar language. These are in fact the key elements of the process we call 'lectio divina'.

It is this spirit that transforms a reading of John from a study of doctrine to an experience of the Lord. His teaching is a way of entering into the movement within the soul that God's love commences, and gives us a new way of viewing reality.

For John, movement or dynamism is fundamental. As you read his writings note how he says God moves and speaks of the movements of the soul which are not so much a conscious decision to enter into the of the Cross of John's name, so much as a surrender to being drawn by God, and as a response to God's enormously attractive power, his captivating energy.

Lectio divina

Mesters makes it easy to review his article, for it concludes by listing ten characteristics within what he calls 'The Attitude of the Faithful Disciple'. Thus, firstly, lectio divina begins with an opening prayer, an invocation of the Holy Spirit. Secondly, there is a slow and attentive reading of the text. Thirdly, there is the movement to a moment of interior silence, to recall what has been read.

---

8   *Walking Side by Side With All Men and Women.* Institutum Carmelitanum, Rome, 1991, p. 86.

Then, fourthly, we look at each phrase. In your reading a text of John's writings, it can be important to discern the rhythm in the text, or the tension or opposition the text contains. Contrasts of sorrow/night can be followed immediately by mention of joy/light. Repeatedly, as he describes the difficulty of the spiritual journey he offers consolation by emphasising the other pole of the tension or the opposition. The master of 'the dark night' is a tower of consoling strength to the traveller.

Opposition is, in another sense, part of John's expertise. He so adeptly portrays, particularly in *The Dark Night of the Ascent of Mount Carmel*, the opposition along the journey that comes from the sinfully dark side of humanity.[9]

When Mesters emphasises, fifthly, that I bring that word into the present, and ponder it in relation to my life, and that, sixthly, I broaden my vision by relating this text to other (biblical and traditional) texts, he is saying something very important to the understanding of lectio divina as contrasted with some form of bible study or some forms of scriptural prayer.

Relating a text to my life is where our reflection, whether it be on a text of scripture or from later church writings that continue to express the tradition out of which even scripture itself was born, enters into the life of the Church. For, as Mesters very beautifully reminds us earlier in his article the bible is not 'my' book, but 'our' book, and, in our search for meaning we must always check our insights with the community to which we belong, and with other

9 William M. Thompson, *Fire and Light, The Saints and Theology*, Paulist Press, New York, 1987. This 'sinfully dark side of humanity' is what Thompson speaks of in chapter 7 entitled: *St John of the Cross as Pneumopathologist: A Mystic's Hermeneutics of Suspicion.*

parts of the Great Tradition which sustains the life of that community. Inevitably we shall have to distinguish between Tradition (also called the Great Tradition) from traditions (or the lesser tradition), a distinction by which we distinguish the essential or unchanging from those traditions that are merely representative of a certain age or a certain culture.

So important is this reference to both the broadening of my vision, and to my life situation with all the complexity of being interrelated with everything within the universe — that Mesters suggests that:

> *when the 'lectio divina' does not reach its goal in our life, the reason is not always our failure to pray, our lack of attention to the faith of the church or our lack of serious study of the text. Oftentimes it is simply our failure to pay attention to the crude and naked reality which surrounds us* (loc. cit. pp. 9-10).[10]

Mesters concludes his description of the faithful disciple by asking the person, seventhly, to read the text again, prayerfully, giving a response to God; eighthly, formulate my commitment in life; ninthly, pray a suitable psalm; and tenthly, choose a phrase which captures the meaning of my prayer, and memorise it.

These are some of the points with which Mesters surrounds the traditional four-step exercise of lectio divina, namely, reading, meditation, prayer, contemplation. This fourth step, contemplation:

> *means having in one's eyes something of the 'wisdom which leads to salvation' (2 Tim 3:15). We begin to see the world and life through the eyes of the poor, through the eyes of*

10 Carlos Mesters O.Carm., *Carmelite* 9, 1991, 5, pp. 9-10.

God. We assume our own poverty and eliminate from our ways of thinking all that smacks of the powerful. We recognise all the many things which we thought were fidelity to God, to the Gospel, and to the Tradition of the Order; 'in reality they were nothing more than fidelity to ourselves and our own interests' (loc. cit. p. 9).[11]

As you begin to use the text of St John of the Cross for 'lectio divina', beginning – as you must – with the literal meaning John intended as the source of the contemporary relevance of that text, you will discover the need to know something of the scholastic method and vocabulary in which St John of the Cross was trained philosophically and theologically.

Any general introduction to the writings of St John of the Cross, for example, such as you will find in the edition of the *Collected Works* edited by Kieran Kavanaugh and Otilio Rodriguez, will satisfy your basic needs. Pay special attention to how John structures the human soul or psyche.

Weaving the fabric of loving God

There are, however, several points that I have found important, which are not always presented in such general introductions.

Firstly, you can see from the index of *The Ascent of Mount Carmel* that John proposes a dark night of the senses, both exterior and interior (Book 1) followed by a dark night of the spirit, namely, the intellect (Book 2), the memory and the will (Book 3). In *The Dark Night of the Soul*, which may be the intended Book 4 of a combined

11   *Ibid.*, p. 9.

Dark Night of the Ascent of Mount Carmel, the author reveals that there is also a passive purification of the same senses and spirit. The careful systemisation of data is typical of scholastic methodology.

Secondly, that systemisation is at one time the product of, and at other times produces, scholasticism's search for deep analysis which breaks the spiritual experience into its components at an abstract level.

What is often overlooked is that the analysis must be synthesised, or re-synthesised at the experiential level of the life situation. And there a clear systemisation is not so evident. The journey to God is not a series of phases where first the senses, and then the spirit, and each of these, first actively and then passively, is purified. Rather life's situations are sometimes actively purificatory, at other times, passively; sometimes the purification of the senses, at other times of the spirit. Individual life situations, as they occur, weave the final fabric of a person loving everything in God without self-concern.

The image of weaving is appropriate, for, as Gregory Burke OCD pointed out in the biographical details of his chapter, *The life and times of St John of the Cross,* John's background is that of the weaver's trade. A colleague, Keith Egan, a member of a group in the USA called the Carmelite Forum has used the image of weaver about John's use of scripture. But we can also use it in regard to the way moments of various forms of purification intermingle in our life. Particularly in regard to what Teilhard de Chardin calls 'the passivities of existence':[12] they may and do occur within life's cycle independent of what stage of active

---

12   F. Kelly Nemek and M.T. Coombs, *O Blessed Night,* Alba, New York, 1991, 114 ff.

purification we have reached. This seems to be implied also in what Constance Fitzgerald OCD has written recently of the passive purification which 'impasse' situations create in our lives.[13] S. Payne OCD[14] addresses the current social justice concern for the oppressed. He rightly points out that these situations, when confronted and sustained in faith and hope and love, are calls for passive purification as well as active confrontation.

Many other daily life situations will be an intermingling of purifications which are active and passive, of the senses and the spirit. The lack of a systemised approach to life's actual journey is partly a verification of 'the Spirit blows where it will' (Jn 3:8) and partly the consequence of the plan being God's not ours.

A final point about the teaching John absorbed from scholasticism concerns a correct understanding of the relationship between the senses and the spirit. The classic understanding of this relationship, as expressed by the great medieval theologian, St Thomas Aquinas, was summarised by the word '*redundantia*', meaning redounding or reverberating. The transformation in the spirit redounds or reverberates in the lower or sensory part of human nature.

Unfortunately, a 17th century influential commentator on the writings of Thomas Aquinas portrayed the process of '*redundantia*' as a suppression of the senses. St John of the Cross antedates that heinous misrepresentation of the human being. In the 40th and final stanza of *The Spiritual Canticle* he writes:

---

13 J. Wolski Conn (ed), Impasse and Dark Night, in *Women's Spirituality: Resources for Christian Development*, Paulist, Mahway, 1986, pp. 287-311.
14 The Dark Night of St John of the Cross: Four Centuries Later, in *Review for Religious*, 1990, 891-900.

No one looked at her,
Nor did Aminadab appear;
The siege was still;
And the cavalry,
At the sight of the waters, descended.[15]

As he explains: creatures cannot discern the happiness of the person immersed in God, and the devil cannot penetrate God's embrace. The stillness of the siege proclaims 'that the passions are put in order according to reason'. The waters, he says, are the spiritual goods and delights that come from the presence of God; the cavalry are the bodily senses, interior and exterior. His comment continues:

'The bride declares that in this state the cavalry descended at the sight of the spiritual waters, because in the state of spiritual marriage the sensory and lower part of the soul is so purified and spiritualised that it recollects the sensory faculties and natural strength so that they may thereby share in and enjoy in their own fashion the spiritual grandeurs which God is communicating in the inwardness of the spirit' (SC 40,5).[16]

The sensory part of the person shares in the spiritual communication.

This is why Ross Collings could write:[17] *'there is a happy irony in the fact that this man, rightly reputed to be one of the great ascetics of Christian tradition, is at the same time a guardian of the sensuous'.* John is neither a killjoy, nor advocate of a warped personality, precisely because the

---

15 Kieran Kavanaugh and Otilio Rodriguez, trans, The Spiritual Canticle 40, in *The Collected Works of St John of the Cross*, ICS Publications, Washington DC, 1979, p. 415.
16 *Ibid.*, 5, pp. 564-565.
17 Ross Collings OCD, Resonant Silences, in *Eureka Street*, Vol 1, No 10, pp. 38-39.

scholastic theory of '*redundantia*' insists that the sense life becomes integrated into the person as God's influence on the spirit rebounds, reverberates, in the senses. Further points about this relation of the senses and the spirit cannot be developed here. I would note, however, that the importance of the notion of '*redundantia*' encapsulates John's appreciation of, and a stage of the journey of, the role of creatures.

First, there is the fact that only the inordinate, voluntary and habitual desire of creatures must be avoided. Secondly, the verse of *The Spiritual Canticle*: 'Tell me has he passed through you' (3,7) is a translation of that verse ('through' rather than 'by') that indicates a clear role for creatures in the ascent to God through ordered rather than disordered desires of the human heart about creatures. Thirdly, he clearly indicates that there comes a stage when creatures *no longer satisfy* (italics author's).

John's teaching about creation was misconstrued by recourse to an inauthentic 17th century explanation of '*redundantia*'. Similarly, John's statement on the drawing of the Mountain: 'Nothing, nothing, nothing and even on the Mount nothing' (of creatures) was considered without relation to what the diagram further says: 'only the glory of God dwells on this mountain' (and we might remember the statement of Irenaeus that 'the glory of God is the human person fully alive in the kingdom' – which is in our midst). The limited explanation of the 'nothing, nothing, nothing [of creatures] even on the Mount' has robbed us of something of what I call the benignity of St John of the Cross' appreciation of God's condescension before our human weakness.

By way of illustrating what I mean by 'benignity' rather than attempt to treat the topic exhaustively, I offer these several examples.

In *The Dark Night of the Soul* (Bk 2 – 12,13), *passim*, John is at pains to describe the benefits that come from this dark night of the senses. He turns to speak of benefits after he has written the awesome passage in *The Dark Night of the Soul* (Bk 1 – 8,2) which says: 'the first purgation is bitter and terrible to the senses.

But nothing can be compared to the second, for it is horrible and frightful to the spirit'. And even in that same chapter, two paragraphs further on (8,4) he mentions 'requirements for entering the *happy* night of the senses' (italics author's). John's narrative or explanation is never going to let us be overwhelmed by 'the night'. This happens countless times in John's works.

Or consider *The Ascent of Mount Carmel* (Bk 2 – 21:1). There John deals with a very current problem, namely the dependence some people have on visions and locutions and other extraordinary phenomena, rather than the naked faith he believes God asks of us. The sequence of his thought is: God is displeased with a person's dependence on visions and revelations; why then does he satisfy the desire some people have for such visions and revelations? John's answer expresses a benignity in God that we, even the Church, fail to display:

> *He does so because of the weakness of the individual who desires to advance in that way. The person could become sad and turn back, or imagine that God is unhappy with him, and become overly afflicted. Or there may be other motives known to God, prompted by the person's weakness and because of which God sees the appropriateness of condescending with such an answer* (loc. cit.).[18]

---

18 Kieran Kavanaugh and Otilio Rodriguez, trans, The Ascent of Mount Carmel II, 21,2, in *The Collected Works of St John of the Cross*, ICS Publications, Washington DC, 1979, p. 173.

That, to me, is an unparalleled statement about the benign God, and an examination of conscience for all of us. The statement is worth copying out and putting on the fridge door, and living it. It seems so appropriate to these times of intolerance and lack of forbearance that is part of a post-Vatican II church.

Finally, – and as an example of the benignity that should exist in all interpersonal relations – let me also recommend to your attentive reading those sections of *The Living Flame* (Bk 3 – 27-62) about spiritual directors. What I am calling the benign spirit of John leads him to remind us that 'it should be known that if a person is seeking God, his Beloved is seeking him much more' (Bk 3 – 28). That's merely one indication of a benign relationship not only with God but also and principally a relationship between director and directee. As I have suggested, these chapters bear reading not only about spiritual direction or soul friends, but also about other relationships in life.

To be God's delight

Most often the benign spirit of John is evident when he wishes to place his teaching about 'the dark night' in proper perspective. And this observation leads me to wonder seriously whether we should give to the phenomena of the dark night the pre-eminence that outlines of, and commentaries upon his experience have done. Admittedly, the experience he describes has given a unique literary presentation; and the memory of his extreme physical sufferings has been kept alive almost as though any 'dark night' would parallel his own terrible sufferings. But, even as we isolate a moment that seems unique in the history of spirituality, we need to recapture the integral experience of John as a Carmelite. In this latter perspective I would ask whether he is the doctor of the dark night, or whether — in the light of his emphasis on purifying disordered appetites (or desires) — he is more aptly described as the doctor of true (accurately ordered) desire. This modifies Gabriel of St Mary Magdalen OCD's use of the title, Doctor of Divine Love; and it reflects the concern in contemporary pastoral theology, especially in the writings of John Paul II, to act in response to the Spirit desiring in the human heart.

The conclusion we must pursue is that the high point of John's *Carmeliteness* is not his emphasis on thorough purification, of the senses and the spirit, both actively and passively. Rather, to be Carmelite is to climb the slopes of Mount Carmel with no need to desire anything because in desiring the All we find everything else. We seek to be God's delight, not God to be our delight.

Veronica Brady IBVM

WHERE CAN YOUR HIDING BE? ST JOHN OF THE CROSS AND THE BASICS OF PRAYER

I have taken for this chapter an epigram from the work of Nicholas Malebrache, the French philosopher who so often found himself overcome by the novelty and the luminousness of thought: 'I will not bring you into a strange country, but I will perhaps teach you that you are a stranger in your own country'.[1] In effect, I want to argue, where we really, that is most deeply live is strange to common sense. This is that 'deep substance of the soul' about which John Follent speaks in Chapter 5, and poetry is one of the best ways to it.

1   Kevin Hart, *The Trespass of the Sign*, Cambridge University Press, Cambridge, 1989, p.xiii.

Spirituality of substance

But before I move to discuss that way, a few words about [the sub-title of this book] *A Spirituality of Substance*. Its implication seems to be that maybe there are spiritualities which lack substance. That is something worth thinking about today when there seems to be a great outburst of 'spirituality' all around us. Here, I think, Marx's critique of 'religion' (not necessarily the same thing as 'faith') must give us pause.

Marx, you will remember, borrowed from Feuerbach for whom conciousness of God was a matter of self-consciousness and knowedge of God self-knowledge; true enough perhaps if properly understood but liable also to turn God into the product of our merely human needs. So Marx was able to attack religion because he saw it merely as the 'generalised theory of the world, its encyclopedic compendium, its logic in popular form, its spiritualistic *point d'honneur* . . . its moral sanction, its solemn complement, its general ground of consolation and justification'.[2]

In his view what people called 'God' was merely a projection of their own emotional and social needs. So rulers invoke God to bless their wars and the rich can regard their riches as signs of God's blessing. God becomes a matter of wish-fulfilment, turned into an idol, and religion becomes a matter of taboo and refuge, product of the fear of punishment and desire for protection and consolation. Adam, after all, was not the last to wish to be 'like God'. We are all in danger of making a God to our own image.

For that reason, the fact that we live in the time of the 'death of God', a time in which for many people in our

2   Lloyd Easton and Kurt Guddat (eds), *Writings of the Young Marx on Philosophy and Society*, Anchor Books, New York, 1967, p. 250.

society religious belief is not really an option, may not be entirely negative. Paul Ricoeur says that the phrase 'God is dead' poses three questions: which 'God' is dead? Who killed him? And what kind of authority comes from the announcement of his death?

An explanation of the thought of St John of the Cross will, I think, give an answer to these questions, though I will leave it to you to deduce them for yourselves. But the title I have taken for this chapter, 'Where can your hiding be?', a line from one of his poems, points to the fact that the answer to the first question is that the living God is not dead but hidden.

Indeed, I would say, that the hiddenness is his special mark. The God who showed himself in the Crucified One and tells us that the way to find ourselves is to lose ourselves can never be an object of our comprehension, much less possession.

Importance of poetry of St John

That brings us to the importance of St John of the Cross and especially of his poetry. Poetry is a special kind of language game, the kind which may be most apt for prayer. All language, of course, is a form of betrayal as well as of revelation.

Neitzche reminds us that the sign is not the thing it stands for, the name is not the thing, the idea is not the deed, the dream is not the action. That is even more true, when we try to speak of God. The opening of St John's Gospel reminds us of this with its magisterial 'In the beginning was the Word'. But the Word is not the same as the word, the human language we use. The Word came to his own home and his own people received him not, though at the same time, paradoxically and generously, to all who received him believed in his name (a word again!) he gave the power to become the children of God, that is, to let our own words give way before the power of the Word. Human language is an echo of God's language but it can never be more than an echo.

Wittgenstein says that we want to establish an order in our knowledge of the use of language, an order with a particular end in view; one out of many possible orders; not the order. Our minds, to borrow from Wittgenstein again, are calloused by rational thinking, unable to be fully sensitive to God's language.[3] As a result of the fall we are no longer entirely in harmony with God, the word is for us 'a chiaroscuro of his presence and absence' (Kevin Hart). We may believe that there is a God, but no word we may ever say about him is ever adequate to express his full reality.

Roland Barthes believes that there comes a point when the dictionary ... comes to a halt with God, who is the keystone in the arch, since God can only be a signified, never a signified: how could God ever mean anything but himself?[4]

A sign is both presence and absence, pointing to what it is not. In the same way, this word and everything in it is a sign of the absence as well as the presence of the God in whom we 'live and move and have our being'. True, he shows himself in Jesus, the perfect sign, but what he shows is also a concealment since what we see is what seems the absence of divinity, the wounded God, St John of the Cross 'wounded here'.

3 Ludwig Wittgenstein, *Philosophical Investigations*, Blackwell, Oxford, 1974, 132, p. 51.
4 Kevin Hart, *op. cit.*, p. 35.

Poetry of prayer

One of the great difficulties of prayer, then, is that it is usually a matter of words. So it is often defined as 'speaking to God', even 'raising the soul to God'. But, we have been arguing, no words can speak to God properly. We can only try to describe him in terms borrowed from human reality. This is where poetry becomes important.

As we have said, poetry is a different kind of language game. Mostly language is expressive, it carries a 'meaning', words point to things, people to ideas which are recognisable. But some language is what we might call indicative, points beyond itself to a gap between the words and what is signified by them and its goal is precisely the experience of this gap.

Poetry is language of this kind. A poem, in Archibald MacLeish's words, 'does not mean but *is*' − just as, to draw a daring analogy, the burning bush of *Exodus* is and is not a bush, burning yet never being consumed. In this sense Wittgenstein tells us that poetry is the form of expression designed for a God who knows what we do not know, sees the whole of each of the infinite series and sees into the human consciousness.[5] It points beyond itself, echoes within us in some sphere of deep resonance, resisting totalisation.

In that sense reading − or writing − poetry is always a form of asceticism, always paradoxical, solitary and yet dialogical. Most of the language of our culture is monological and one-dimensional, pretending to possess truth ready-made. But poetry points beyond itself to that which comes to us by means of language.

5   Ludwig Wittgenstein, *op. cit.*, p.2451.

... *Words strain,*
Crack and sometimes break, under the burden,
Under the tension, slip, slide, perish,
Decay with imprecision, will not stay in place,
Will not stay still. Shrieking voices
Scolding, mocking, or merely chattering
Always assail them.

(T.S. Eliot, Burnt Norton V, *Four Quartets*)[6]

Yet the words of poetry can also for this reason be an occasion of grace. Forming themselves, as Bakhtin finely says, in an atmosphere of what has already been spoken (the Word), the words of poetry are at the same time determined by what they cannot say, but what they most deeply long for. Nothing has life except by this living Word which continually calls forth our words but remains always open-ended, unfinalised, tensed at the entrance to the tomb, our dying to our human perception and understanding, waiting for the resurrection.

St John's poetry model of prayer

This bring us, then, to the poetry of St John of the Cross as a model of prayer. Since I am neither a theologian nor a scholar of his poetry it seems best merely to list a set of reflections about this poetry.

First, there is the fact that for most of us it is necessary to read these poems in translation, intensifying the gap between the words and what they point to. It is a disadvantage but also an advantage to the extent that it increases

---

6   T.S. Eliot, Burnt Norton V, in *Four Quartets*, Faber & Faber, London, 1964, p. 194.

our sense of the ways in which, as Eliot has it, 'Words, after speech reach/into the silence'. This sense grows with the realisation that these are poems which began in prison. Imprisoned in his small cell in Toledo, St John of the Cross went inwards, listening and hearing what could otherwise not be heard:

> *In darkness, hid from sight*
> *I went by secret ladder, safe and sure ...*
> *... No one to see my flight,*
> *No other guide or light*
> *Save one that in my heart burned bright as day.*[7]

Prayer begins at the point of helplessness, stillness. Being 'confined within a nut-shell it is possible to become "King of infinite space"'. All that is necessary is faith and hope and love, faith in the God who calls, saying, 'I am the Lord thy God who brought thee out of the land of Egypt, out of the house of bondage' (Lev 26:13), speaking to us of resurrection and liberation even as we remain suspended between his presence and absence, drawing us by longing and revealing himself as 'the wounded heart'. The opening of the poems, then, begins in the dark, in powerlessness, replacing the certainties of overconfident belief with this longing.

Yet in his small cell the saint also learned about love of this world. His poetry echoes the secular love poetry of his day as well as that great love poem, the *Song of Songs* in Scripture and, I like to think, secular love songs which he may have heard sung in the street outside his cell, using them with complete freedom, turning themes he turned everything to the purposes of prayer, mixing the sacred and

---

7   John of the Cross, The Dark Night, in *Centred on Love, the Poems of St John of the Cross*, E. Marjorie Flower OCD, trans, private circulation.

the profane, the courtly and the popular. He does not think
it sinful to let the world speak or to celebrate God's crea-
ting. As Moltmann remarks, 'the God who was crucified
not between two candlesticks on the altar but between two
thieves on the place of the skull',[8] is no remote God
incapable of feeling but one who has committed himself
entirely to us and to our world as the 'lone young shepherd'
as the saint figures him 'far from comfort and in deep
distress' and 'a deep wound of love had torn his heart'.

My next point is to do with memory. At first these poems
were not written down (they could not be since he did not
have pen or paper), but remembered. In his prison, the
memory of all he had known and loved, the flowers, and
fountains, mountains and gardens, shepherds and their
flocks, love songs and music, returned to him. Our society
lives in the instantaneous present. But the time of faith is
the time of memory on the one hand, the recollection of
God's great deeds in us and in his people, and of hope,
desire for his final triumph. This memory and hope make
us love the world, but love it in God. Thus St John of the
Cross' spirituality is not isolated away from the world. He
plunges fully into life, seeing it as God's gift:

> *My Love's a mountain range,*
> *deep lonely valley, wooded down below,*
> *far islands, rare and strange,*
> *streams singing as they flow,*
> *whisper of loving breezes, soft and low.*[9]

There is nothing disembodied about this spirituality. But
the reality of the world is spiritual rather than spatial. It
is holy because God is holy and has made us holy in our

8   Jurgen Moltmann, *The Church in the Power of the Spirit*, SCM,
     London, 1988, p. 246.
9   John of the Cross, The Spiritual Canticle, *op. cit.*

own measure with the lack of praising him in a thorough creation.

For St John of the Cross, what is beautiful, then, leads to God. It also increases hunger for God since, as Kevin Hart has observed in another context, 'without the presence of God, in paradise or on earth, there can be no hope of understanding ourselves, others or texts. One would be lost in a maze of signs without the possibility of distinguishing true from false'[10]. Prayer therefore involves the unity of the inward and outward, the individual and the social. Echoing the literary forms, even sometimes the conventions of feeling of his own time, intensifies the hunger. Prayer is not so much a matter of speaking to God but listening to him at work in the world as well as in the self, listening to what the Spirit, more intimate to ourselves than our selves, is saying within. This is the source of all true obedience as its root meaning, which derives from the notion of listening (*audire*), reminds us.

Phases of prayer

The time framework of the poems, to consider it next, reflects the three phases of prayer. As far as the past is concerned, the poems look backward, reflecting on the great deeds of God's love, in the Old Testament, especially as they are expressed in the *Song of Songs*, in the New Testament, especially in the crucifixion, that greatest and all-embracing deed of love and showing of God's all-encompassing generosity and mercy to us. In the present, they celebrate the presence of the Lord in his Spirit,

10   Kevin Hart, *op. cit.*

moving through this world, animating and sanctifying it, making it for us a series of signs of his love, moving in our hearts and in the church as a community of prayer and loving. Finally, in the future, there is the expectation of the coming of the Lord, which is the source of the longing which pervades the poem.

By definition, therefore, prayer involves a sense of incompleteness and thus of longing, the key trope of the poems. The self in them is always in movement towards the one she loves, never entirely coincides with herself and never living entirely where she is in the sense that she is always on the way to some further intensity of presence, living

> ... *with no life of my own*
> *so filled with longing love that I*
> *am dying that I do not die,* [11]

longing to be 'lost to myself at last' yet constantly finding the source of love, the 'living flame, compelling/yet tender past all telling' within 'the secret centre of my soul'. Put in more prosaic terms, self-awareness means realisation of the difference, this distance and therefore of this longing, 'dying that I do not die'.

It is this sense of loss, I think, which for all their apparent simplicity makes the poems so difficult. Often, for instance, it is not clear who is addressing what about whom. The absent bridegroom and the hidden bride are shadowy figures, their voices sometimes apparently interchangeable – that, of course, is what they long for, perfect unity, though it also can never be achieved in this life. What is being said is what cannot be said, does not make rational sense, the certainty that the living spring flows, for

11   John of the Cross, stanzas of The Soul That Suffers With Longing to See God, *op. cit.*

instance although it cannot be seen, and is only found at night in darkness rather than light. The goal is to go beyond anything that can be known, . . . into an unknown land unknowing, (and to) stay there 'knowing naught', beyond the power of human thought. Thus in stanza four the self seems to lose control, and being unable to suffer any longer the soul begs him to reveal himself and show his beauty, to stay her with the vision thereof, and thus loose her from the flesh (since she cannot see him in the flesh and have fruition of him as he desires).[12]

The highest point in this sense is also the lowest, humility, the truthful realisation that we are not in charge of our lives but beholden to the one who draws us to him to complete us.

This interweaving of activity and passivity gives the poetry this complex tension. But it also expresses the truth of our relationship with God, the 'One who comes', who keeps on 'going on ways to himself', as Eberhard Jüngel finely says.[13] In this relationship, God can never be known as an object.

In that we know God, we know that we are already known – hence in *The Spiritual Canticle* the inversion of the story of narcissus as the image which appears in the crystal spring appears as that of the beloved, not of the self. The more we announce the call to prayer, the more we become aware that we have ourselves not as a procession but as an offering.

---

12 John of the Cross, Commentary on The Living Flame, stanza 4, in *The Complete Works of St John of the Cross*, E. Allison Peers, trans, Burns & Oates, London, 1964.
13 Eberhard Jüngel, *God as the Mystery of the World*, William B. Erdmans, Grand Rapids, Michigan, 1983, p. 9.

Love as a wandering

This brings us to the next observation about the poetry, the importance of the idea of love as a journey or, better perhaps, a wandering. In Spanish the word used is *vagan*. In English it also means 'to be vacant' or to 'employ'. In this sense it describes all those who serve God, the 'young maidens', for instance, who 'follow, yearning to find, the sandal-prints where you have trod', wandering the world in search of him.

There is always something more to desire because God is not someone who has love but who *is* love, so that before him even our most intense love is emptiness. Before him, each of us is always the wanderer on the way to self, beyond all the words there is always the Word, beyond the language of creatures something which remains to be said and yet cannot be said in their language which must remain always a kind of stammering:

All those who come and go
freely, speak of your graciousness, but they
wound worst of all, and though
it leaves me dying, stay
and stammer − what? − I know no way to say.[14]

Creatures merely stammer, talk like children, cannot convey what they have to say. In the saint's words, they 'seem to be expressing the grandeurs of God but are unable to express them perfectly ... [and] fall far short of making them understand'. Yet what they are stammering also, the saint says, 'leaves me dying' because they point to a trace of the beloved and thus point us into the silence, into the 'unknown land' in which

14   John of the Cross, *The Spiritual Canticle*, 7, *op. cit.*

> *... all (he) knew*
> *before is gone and lost from view*
> *as worthless now. He knows not why his knowledge rises*
>   *constantly*
> *but he remains as knowing naught*
> *far, far beyond all human thought.*[15]

Prayer, then, is movement. As the saint puts it in his commentary the 'clearly imprinted trace of God which is revealed to the soul and which it has to follow' also the calls of faith.

Journey through darkness

This brings us to the next point, the heroism of prayer. As it is described in the poems, the soul's journey echoes the heroic mood of the sixteenth century, the age of the conquistadors. In search of love the bride is also prepared to go

> *beyond the mountains, lowlands, far away*
> *no fear of wild beast know*[16]

to cross frontiers, defy fortresses and 'dread rulers of the watches of the night'. As the world becomes a place of unlikeness it becomes more dangerous as well as more painful, calling beyond the 'utmost range/or understanding' to live by

> *this unknown knowledge, darkly taught*
> *beyond the power of human thought.*[17]

---

15 John of the Cross, *After an Ecstasy*, 5, *op. cit.*
16 John of the Cross, *The Spiritual Canticle*, 3, *op. cit.*
17 John of the Cross, *After an Ecstasy*, 7, *op. cit.*

Precisely because the genuine life of the spirit takes place at the point of non-coincidence between self and desire it is risky, demanding the courage to go within into the 'deep caverns of the soul', trusting only in the light of the living flame of love. The call comes from within the self but also far beyond the self and is a call to go forth. To say 'here I am', is to say 'I hear', hearing only though longing to see and trusting in the call.

As the poetry makes abundantly clear, that involves a journey through darkness. The way to the All must mean having nothing. I must forget who I am if I am to listen to and be guided by the Other who calls me into what must forever be beyond me – hence the images of kingly power and of excess of beauty which surround the beloved in the poem. As Thomas Merton has pointed out, in comparison with Being, created being is not.

God *is* not, and where he is is nowhere in our terms. 'If you go all the way to Being', as Heidegger said, 'You get no-thing'.

This, of course, is the mystery. He is found and we in him only when we have lost ourselves, given ourselves away in love, fidelity and complete generosity under the guidance of the Spirit who calls, the living flame which heals by burning and gives light by the way of darkness. Then, however, a whole new world opens out, creation transfigured, mountain ranges,

> *deep lonely valleys, wooden down below,'*
> *far islands, rare and strange,*
> *streams singing as they flow,*
> *whisper of loving breezes, soft and low.*[18]

---

18   John of the Cross, *The Spiritual Canticle*, 15, *op. cit.*

The world is seen now as it really is in the mystery of the true God. A great expanse opens out, the freedom which comes from being enthralled by God, as Thomas Merton says, that being with the one who cannot be seen is to be nowhere, to be no one, but lost, forgotten, to live by his power and wisdom, drawn into his wedding feast.

At this point, all language falls away. Even poetry is completely inadequate. All that is left is love, and in love presence overcomes representation, what matters is not to speak, not even to think, but to Love:

Filled with delight to be Love's prey
I feel his flame consume, and see
nothing is left, for rapidly
the whole of me is burned away.[19]

A means to truth

Nevertheless, to return to the point at which we began, poetry is the least inadequate kind of language to express this experience because it is language which points beyond itself. In poetry, as in the spiritual life, meaning is not a static set of points or an organised framework, but a movement from one to the other. It is thus a matter of transformation, of translating words into experience.

It is also dialogical rather than monological, a matter of symbols rather than mere signs, pointing beyond the maze of signs to the ultimate signification which can never be fully signified by any words of ours but which is nevertheless echoed in them, analogously. In St John of the Cross' words:

19 John of the Cross, *With a Divine Meaning*, 4, *op. cit.*

Thou livest not where thou livest. The soul lives in that which it loves rather than in the body because it has not life in the body but rather in the spirit. Love gives it to the body and lives in that which it lives.

It is God who not only gives life to all but ultimately speaks in all that is spoken and speaks most intensely where language is at its most intense.

Poetry matters for prayer, therefore, because it unsettles settled habits of language which pretends to possess a ready-made truth and allows us to live as it were by a kind of alibi, living elsewhere than the true centre of myself, without taking responsibility for myself, and the call of love which comes to us. St John of the Cross' poems, then, become a means to truth, taking us away from the confidence of mere commentary about God to the experience of him, undermining words to replace them with longing, drawing us beyond ourselves. The world they set out so vividly before us is at the one and the same time everywhere and nowhere. In this way they remind us of the essential deficiency not only of all created things but even of prayer itself as well as poetry. As St John of the Cross says, in the evening of our lives we will be judged by love. So, too, will poetry.[20]

---

20 *See* Les Murray, ed, *Anthology of Australian Religious Poetry*, Blackburn, Victoria, CollinsDove, 1991, p. 98.

John Follent OCD

NEGATIVE EXPERIENCE AND CHRISTIAN GROWTH

Contrary to the expectations of many potential readers, St John of the Cross is one of the most 'available' of saints. Our aim now is to give some indication of how this is so by speaking of his doctrine in the context of a very common type of Christian experience which is generally perceived as difficult and problematic. One of John's greatest qualities is to be able to show clearly the light and positive value that are present in aspects of experience which most regard as negative or even potentially destructive. Nor is the experience we will be discussing something unusual or off the main track of 'ordinary Christian life'. On the contrary, we will maintain that it is, or eventually becomes, for many persons the habitual way of their everyday Christian journey. It is therefore of considerable pastoral significance.

All spiritual life involves an alternation of light and darkness, consolation and desolation, the kataphatic (by way of manifestation or appearing) and the apophatic (by way of non-manifestation and obscurity). In order not to lose perspective on what follows, we must bear in mind that John writes as much in the kataphatic context as he does in the apophatic. There is no morbidity or exaltation of suffering for suffering's sake in his writings. His passionate engagement with the beauty of God's creation is evident in his poetry, yet it must also be said that he invests suffering in Christian life with great potential and actual value. Given, then, that there is a necessary alternation in the process of human growth, and that innocent and unsought suffering seems to be a well-nigh universal fact in life,[1] it is clear that any account of spiritual life which does not attempt to come to terms with such suffering, and somehow show its place in the overall process of spiritual life and growth, is worthless. If we see no positive Christian meaning in periods of difficulty and trial, we generally fall away into discouragement and despair.

There is also the problem of the ambiguity of all human experience. Whatever subjective value we may attribute to an element of our experience, questions still remain about its true meaning in the larger context of Christian reality. This is particularly so in the realm of contemplative and mystical prayer where the reality of God as Absolute Mystery is encountered experientially. St John remarks:

> *Truly thou art a hidden God. Hence it is to be noted that, however lofty are the communications of a soul with God in this life, ... and however high and exalted is its*

---

1   By 'suffering' in the present context, we do not mean pain (physical, emotional, mental or spiritual) which is being coped with. Rather, what is meant here is pain which is not being coped with, mastered, or contained in the sense that it, and the problem which underlies it, are resolved. For those who have had long experience of the second, the first aproximates more to consolation!

knowledge of Him, they are not God in His essence nor have aught to do with Him. For in truth He is still hidden from the soul, and therefore it ever beseems the soul, amid all these grandeurs, to consider Him as hidden, and to seek Him as One hidden, saying: 'Whither hast thou hidden Thyself?' For neither is a sublime communication of Him or a sensible revelation of His presence a sure testimony of His gracious presence, nor is aridity or the want of all these things in the soul a testimony of His absence from it. For which cause says the Prophet Job: 'If He comes to me I shall not see Him; and if He goes away, I shall not understand Him'[2] (Spiritual Canticle 1:3).

Example of a common problem

Let us now take a hypothetical example of a common problem or crisis in contemplative Christian life. We assume that the kind of person we are considering is serious about seeking God and living in his presence.

It is also of great importance that he or she is more concerned with desiring oneness with God rather than having feelings about God, or thoughts and meditations about God. This person just wants God — in a kind of naked sheer immediacy — and doesn't *know* what is *meant* by this. There is just the wanting of God himself and, in principle, a lack of satisfaction with anything less. (We say *in principle* because some degree of compromise will always be present in the normal run of cases.)

2   The text of St John of the Cross used throughout this chapter is taken from *The Complete Works of St John of the Cross*, E. Allison Peers, trans and ed, Wheathampstead, Hertfordshire, 1974.

Furthermore, we may assume that God has satisfied these longings in part through the gift of various forms of passive prayer — i.e. forms of prayer not essentially dependent on one's own efforts. Such prayer may involve great *light* and consolation in the understanding, and great satisfaction (a sense of loving and being loved) in the deep levels of will and desire. It may, on the other hand, involve a less intense and drier, yet ready facility in simply being with God *mindlessly*, i.e. without any intellectual contents; and *feelinglessly*, i.e. simply desiring God in a peaceful emptiness, consoled by the certainty that in this very *mindless* simple prayer one is supported by God and graced by God.

> *That which aforetime the soul was gaining gradually through its labour or meditation upon particular facts has now through practice, ... become converted and changed into a habit and substance of loving knowledge, of a general kind, and not distinct or particular as before. Wherefore when it gives itself to prayer, the soul is now like one to whom water has been brought, so that he drinks peacefully without labour and is no longer forced to draw the water through the aqueducts of past meditations and forms and figures*[3] (Dark Night 2:1,1).

It is of capital importance to stress at this point that the kind of contemplation adverted to above does not have its centre of gravity primarily in the psyche and feelings. The psyche may be involved, but psychic contents do not constitute the primary dimension of the experience.

The contemplative light and love seem to originate from a region of spiritual being anterior to psychological and conceptual consciousness, from what some spiritual

3   *Dark Night,* 2:1,1, *op. cit.*

writers call the *fine point of the soul* or the *ground of the soul*. In fact it is precisely in contemplative experience that one becomes aware of and lives from this region.

John calls this region the *substance of the soul* (D.N. 6:5; 13:3). So profoundly substantial is this region that any consolation experienced there is a spiritual abundance — conversely, desolation experienced there is experienced as annihilation. For John, this substance is the locus of union with God.

Problems begin when a previous facility for the *general indistinct* contemplative knowledge goes. What results is a kind of emptiness in the area of faith. There is no capacity for returning to either the passive contemplative awareness, or fruitful reflection and meditation, during the time of prayer.

Outside of prayer fruitful reflection is certainly possible and even necessary. Theology is possible and the insights proper to theology are experienced as fruitful. But the moment one turns to prayer that sense of fruitfulness goes. One does not have the sense of being able to *enter into* the realities of faith, or to be *one* with whatever theological reality one is considering as was often the case before. One is dealing with the husk and cannot break through to the pith. There is an acute sense of separation accompanied by anguish as distinct from a previous kind of faith knowledge which seemed to be grounded in an experiential, even if obscure, incorporation into the very reality of Christ.

There is, of course, inevitable anxiety as to why this should be the case. The key words here are *participation* and *incorporation* and it is precisely the reality that these words signify which has to be deepened and further confirmed.

Trial by faith

This obscurity of faith can intensify to the point where the objects of faith seem to be unreal and faith itself is sometimes experienced as being under threat. Indeed there may be a conviction that one has little or no faith. This is graphically described by St Thérèse of Lisieux in her autobiography under the title *Trial of Faith*.[4] To turn to God in prayer was to turn into a void into which she spoke what were felt to be empty words of belief. This trial continued for years with occasional *flashes* of light until her death. These periodic *flashes*, or inner illuminations are a not uncommon element of the condition of which we speak. They may involve a palpable experience of the light of faith, whereby saturated by an inner illumination one seems to penetrate into the profound depths of the reality underlying Christian truths, or into the utter loveliness of the luminosity of God's grace present in a fellow Christian. Again these moments of light may intensify into what St Thérèse has called *intellectual visions*.

By this we mean the inner apprehension of both the presence and the substance of a reality of faith (for example the Trinity, Christ, Our Lady) which is received without any accompanying image or precept. However, in the case which we are considering, such consolations generally go quickly and the desolation which follows them is experienced as more intensely deprivative in the light of them.

Such a profound assault upon the area of faith necessarily reverberates into other areas of spiritual consciousness. For example, one's previous modes of self-possession or one's habitual sense of having an identity in God are disrupted.

4   John Clarke OCD (trans and ed), St Thérèse of Lisieux, *Story of a Soul*, ICS Publications, Washington, DC, 1976, pp. 205-229.

Inner spiritual resources upon which one could habitually rely no longer seem to apply. Whereas before there was perhaps a sense of integration in Christ and a certain spiritual confidence, now there is disorientation and emptiness.

There is no sense of being able to rest upon either God or created things. Nothing seems to be able to provide support, and if this condition continues for a long time anxiety intensifies greatly. Frantic efforts are made to fill up the emptiness – distraction or work but these do not meet the real issue which is taking place primarily in the *substance of the soul*. There are inevitably temptations to despair of God and his goodness, and perhaps this is the most dangerous temptation encountered in the spiritual life. We are reminded of the stories of the early desert fathers who spoke of being tempted to blasphemy and rage with God. Put simply, there is an experience of being undone, and the more God's mercy and love are active, the experience will be that of being utterly and completely undone.

Yet even though faith and trusting hope are put under pressure, and may even be perceived to be absent, one continues to live off them and in them. One has left Egypt and has not yet learned to savour the hidden manna, since food from God is being provided.

The reality of life with God is a reality of loving and being loved. Our hypothetical person once had an habitual sense of love for God and of being loved by God. In the context of the problem of which we speak, pressure is placed on both sides of this equation. All of one's spiritual activities of love now seem empty; one must do them if one is not to be overwhelmed by negativity, but however well one tries to do them, an anguished sense of separation from God continues.

Because of the absence of light one is driven back onto
one's own darkness without God, and there may be a strong
sense of the ambiguity and basic flux running through all
one's religious aspirations and activities. In the light of
previous experiences of profound loving incorporation into
God; of being overwhelmed by God's communications of
love; of experiences of having one's own spiritual acts
informed and transfigured in the light of God's own Spirit
and the form of Christ – the present situation seems
inexplicable. In the mild form, one has the sense of simply
having nothing to offer God. In the more intense mode
there is an experience of absence of love which is at times
overwhelming – a sense of being unlovable in God's sight
and unloved by God – perhaps even abandoned by God.
Such perceived separation from God may become a constant anguish and a continual background to active Christian life, but it is really in private prayer and liturgical life
that it comes to the foreground. Many come to dread the
time of prayer.

The experience of grace

The experience of grace at this point may be said to be
hidden but it is very real. It is focused in the desire such
persons find in themselves to persevere and keep going. It
is also manifested in the profound conviction that Christ
is everything, and that in spite of the cost of discipleship
being often more than one can bear, there are no regrets
and it is all worth it.

Such experiences of grace as desire and conviction will
be very real yet quite unfelt. One will not feel like persevering, yet one will because the strength is given to the
substance if not the psyche. One will frequently be tempted

conceptually against the conviction of the value of perseverance in close discipleship, yet the conviction will remain in spite of thoughts to the contrary.

We have already adverted to the distinction between what St John of the Cross calls the substance of the soul and the areas of conceptual and psychic life, and stressed its importance. It is quite possible, and even usual, for us to perceive the division, particularly at prayer. There may be turmoil and trouble in both mind and psyche, yet underneath this, one may be quite peaceful. That is, provided one's religious intentionality is not centred in one's psyche.

The more one is able to *let go* and abandon all psychic and conceptual contents, the more aware one becomes of this deeper substance of oneself and of the way in which God may reveal his presence there. Yet this *awareness* need not register in the more superficial dimensions of consciousness at all. Even thoughts about God can be a distraction from a deeper and different knowledge of God, whilst *getting in touch* with one's feelings about God at times of prayer can also block off a deeper participation in God's reality, cause positive harm, and impede progress. The less conscious we are at the time of prayer the better.

The distinction made here has practical importance in the life of prayer, and in times of trial, if at all possible, one should have recourse to this deeper substantial level. However, this is frequently not possible since it is precisely from the *substance of the soul* that the darkness of which we are speaking here is originating. If what we have said so far is an accurate statement of a rather common experience of Christian life, how then is it to be understood and interpreted?

When John speaks of the active Divine presence (love) in the substance of the soul, he frequently uses the Spanish word *embestir* which means 'to assail' (*Dark Night* II, 5, 5; *Living Flame* 1:19,22,25,35; *Spiritual Canticle* 13:3f). As we said above, this assailing or overwhelming presence can be experienced as contemplative expansion or enrichment of conscious faith life. But John also maintains that such active loving presence of God can assail the person at a deeply substantial level so as to produce the opposite, i.e. an experience of great poverty.

Both experiences of *richness* and *poverty* under God are given as elements in God's transforming action of love — conversion — but conversion at the most profound level and as passively undergone. One is converted, changed, transformed by God's presence and not by one's own proper activities. Within this assailing, *connaturality* with God's Holy Spirit is intensified radically, and that in us which is in opposition to God, or contrary to the form of Christ, becomes increasingly painful and indeed eventually intolerable. The unconverted un-Christlike elements of self appear as poverty in the light of God's nearness.

> *The weaknesses and miseries which the soul had aforetime hidden and set deep within it (which aforetime it neither saw nor felt) are now seen and felt by it, by means of the light and heat of the Divine fire. ... For at this season — oh, wondrous thing! — there arise within the soul contraries against contraries, the things of the soul against the things of God, which assail the soul; and some of these ... bring the others to light, and they make war in the soul, striving to expel each other in order that they may reign within it. ... So the soul has to suffer the existence of two contraries within it. For as this flame is of brightest light, and assails the soul, its light shines in the darkness of the soul, which is dark as the light is bright; and then the soul is conscious of its vicious natural darkness, which sets itself against the supernatural light, and it is not conscious of the super-*

natural light, because it has it not within itself as it has its own darkness, and the darkness comprehends not the light[5] (Living Flame 1,22).

Another important factor which enters into our considerations is the issue of *mastery*. We may say that another cause of the spiritual and psychological pain of contemplation is the breakdown of effective mastery and self-projection in the spiritual life. There is an erosion of the sense of being able to deal with God on our terms.

The new contemplative mode of being with God, of which we are speaking here, is the reverse of any kind of mastery or projection. Rather, it is a kind of receptive passivity, an abandonment into God, whereby one loses and moves beyond the old sense of reality and self that was in place — a sense of reality and self that was largely self-constructed — and begins to take on in a far more radical manner the form of Christ. By *form of Christ* we mean the totality of those aspects and qualities of the reality of Christ which set him off from all other persons, which constitute him as uniquely himself, and which must be grasped and apprehended if he is to be really known and understood. It is precisely to the degree that one is given this *form of Christ* by God that one participates in the life of grace. The form of Christ may be spoken about accurately in the abstract (but quite necessary) mode of theology in such a way that the various elements of the form are clearly ordered one to the other.

But what we are speaking of here is not abstract, it is quite concrete and particular, and hence takes on the character of a certain disorder and unpredictability. In so far as one is willing to submit as peacefully as is possible to

5 *Living Flame*, 1, 22, *op. cit.*

this unpredictability in the following of Christ, without laying down one's own ground rules and conditions, one grows into a harmony; into those dimensions of the reality of God's love in Christ which lie beyond what we can comprehend, experience or place in a systematic order.

We also grow into a harmony with God's new way of communicating his love and reality. The difference is that between changing oneself and being changed by another. Such expropriation or displacement is a benchmark of the quality and meaning of Christian love and indeed of all true love.

In a similar manner, when we are present to a truly great work of art, we approach it in homage. We are concerned to let it overwhelm us, and if we are to take it into ourselves we must be completely at its disposal. We do not, above all, in any way try to *reduce* it to our own parameters. On the contrary, we are willing to be receptive to something greater than ourselves. We grow up to it and into it. In all true human love, this desire to lose oneself in the other's form, to take the other's form into oneself or be *informed* by the other is paramount.

When such a basic characteristic of Christian life is absent, and we find ourselves largely *pulling our own strings* by means of techniques or whatever other method, something is radically wrong. In the realm of faith this point is made sharply by Hans Urs von Balthasar.

Experience of faith implies that the object of faith offers itself precisely when and in so far as the person renounces his own ability to grasp and comprehend, and surrenders and delivers himself over to what is to be believed. This is why the believer cannot desire, without contradiction, to register this self-surrender as such in a pychological manner, not even in the unique case in which the object — God himself in his revelational self-surrender — wants to indwell both the person that surrenders and his act of faith. ... Now, by act of faith and surrender what is meant in the Bible and in reality is an act of self-surrendering love to God. For this reason, it is not erroneous to say that the lover in all things renounces what is his own and desires to clear all available space in himself for the beloved; the lover, therefore, embraces as his own the experience which is the beloved's and, on the contrary, he no longer desires to have within himself *what a non-lover would call* his own experience, *but to have it* only in the beloved.[6]

Now in so far as contemplation is an experience of faith, it will therefore necessarily take on the quality of faith decribed here — expropriation. The primary indication that this is happening is when a person is stripped of all guarantees which are rooted in the self, and begins to live on the faith, trust and love that they have in the other — God. In practical terms, this expropriation in faith will involve an immediate experience of God as sheer Mystery in the strictest sense. The closeness of this Mystery — its indwelling — will more and more characterise the periods of prayer and will displace all *specified* mental and psychic activity. That is, it will displace all thinking and perception of God as an *object*. There will be times when this expropriation, or union with God in Mystery, is becoming more profound, that it will be distressing, as we read in St Thérèse's account of her prayer. But in a curious *supra-sensible* way often it will also be peaceful and indeed joyful. One will be aware in the unfelt substance of oneself that what one really wants is God and nothing but God.

6   Hans Urs von Balthasar, *The Glory of The Lord*, A Theological Aesthetics, Vol I: Seeing the Form, T and T Clark, Edinburgh, 1982, p. 257 f.

In so far as one slowly accepts the reality of God's loving presence as expropriation, and is willing to consign all of one's life and *experience* to God, one will begin to discover a strange fullness in the emptiness. While there may be nothing specific registering in one's consciousness at the times of prayer, in this *nothing* there is in fact *everything*, and faith lived at this level is enough. Degrees of darkness or light are all the same and one loses the taste for various kinds of psychological registration. Also, in so far as one is prepared to abandon all projections and projects that involve self-constitution before God, and consign oneself to God in an ongoing act of trust that allows oneself to be constituted rather than the opposite, one is learning something of the reality of Christian love. For to consign oneself freely to the expropriating action of God's love is to love God. The complete simplicity and acceptance of God's ways is described wonderfully by Thomas Merton in an article on the solitary life.[7] To refer to our *problem experience*, it is clear that given what we outline here being the actual state of affairs, feelings of *not having faith* are merely the obverse side of the expropriation process and the displacement of a conceptual or imaginative habit of faith by something deeper and much more substantial. In fact, such a person has great faith in spite of all perceptions to the contrary, and a good spiritual adviser can readily see this.

Growth in God

Also, in so far as growth in God means being stripped of all guarantees which are rooted in the self, and demands

7   Thomas Merton, *The Monastic Journey*, Sheed Andrews and McMeel, Inc., Kansas City, 1977, p. 159.

an existential shift towards the placing of one's trust and hope (one's life) upon the guarantees that God provides in Christ alone, and all that pertains to Christ, it is hardly surprising that such growth will present difficulties. The abandonment of self-mastery and the taking on of a radical dependence on God will necessarily be accompanied by a sense of being undone or being annihilated, yet such an anxiety is quite ungrounded. In fact, the discovery that one can no longer find one's guarantees in oneself may indeed be a sign that progress in the life with God is finally being achieved.

Another curious dimension of the problem which we noted – the sense of separation, perceptions of radical difference, of having nothing to offer God, or a strong awareness of one's own poverty in the area of love of God; all of these may be no more than an accurate perception of the truth in the light of deep involvement with God, and should be a cause for peace rather than disturbance.

We are reminded here of St Ignatius' remarks to the effect that the greater the growth into similarity with the ways and things of God, the greater the correlative sense of dissimilarity from them. Yet the presence of a fundamental conviction of the meaning and worthwhileness of an unconditional following of Christ, and the discovery in oneself of the energy and willingness to push on through the trials of faith and hope, actually indicate the presence of a considerable love for God. Nor should it be surprising if prayer, in the sense of *experience* of union with God, becomes at such times the most crucifying aspect of one's life. Nevertheless, this very anguish that arises from an awareness of lack of union with God has its basis in love. If we did not love God we would hardly care if we were united with him or not.

We have spoken so far almost entirely in the context of

the apophatic and loving engagement of a person in the
Mystery of God, strictly speaking, and of some of the
strange paradoxes that result from this. But what are we
to say to the Lord Jesus Christ in this context?

Much could be said, but we content ourselves here with
merely pointing out that as this more profound dwelling
within God's mysterious and inconceivable loving presence
progresses, and the more one is immersed in the peaceful
(or unpeaceful) obscurity of which we speak, the more the
person of Jesus Christ is apprehended as the only form in
the created order of being which is apposite to and is
appropriately expressive of what one *knows* immediately in
the depths of oneself. That is to say, from the very emptiness of prayer, one *sees* the Lord as being beyond worth and
as being incomparably lovely. The contours of his being
appear as simply and absolutely *right*.

He is also perceived as infinitely exceeding whatever of
him one can take in, or somehow specify, and this perception has as its ground the dark and obscure expropriation
in faith, trust and love, of which we have been speaking.
This *excess*, which is perceived out of the very ground of
faith, is what draws us on in the hope of an ever recurring
and deepening *seeing more* and loving more of what we see.

It must be stressed again that such *seeing* will not have
its centre of gravity in the psychic or conceptual regions
of spiritual consciousness, nor will it be necessarily *clear*
or consoling. Neither will it necessarily take away the
darkness and pain we have been speaking of. Yet it will
mean something, it will be sustaining and it is an incompar-
able blessing. Furthermore, it may also be said that from
Christ, and the light that makes itself manifest in him, one
perceives something of the contours and meaning of what
one *experiences* most profoundly about oneself, others and

the world as such. Inner experience, especially if apophatic, and the reality of Christ have somehow become one.

Other people's experience

Finally, we turn to the reality of other people in our lives. That we are dependent on other people in some way for every significant move we make in the direction of God goes without saying. It is also true that the one unfailing litmus test of how we are faring in the life with God is the inevitable correlative of how we are situated in our lives with others.

But in the light of our considerations, we may certainly say that precisely from the perspective of suffering and difficulty in expropriation, one often sees the beauty that God has placed in others. Just as the contours of Christ are *seen* more truly from the darkness of apophatic prayer, so the light of God, and specific graces and contours arising from this light of God, will be perceived in others.

One sees, with a simple clarity, elements of the Christ form that God has placed in others. This will not be perceived in all cases! But if it is seen in a few, it is sufficient to revolutionise our attitudes to people in general.

Where this beauty and goodness are seen, as Christ is perceived as being beyond worth, so too are others. Furthermore, precisely as a result of the experience of *losing one's life* that we have called expropriation, one may discover in oneself a deep compassion for the sufferings of others, even complete strangers, and an anguish at the often apparently destructive negativity in their lives. Nor is this something constructed or *put on* in some controlled or managed way.

What we speak of here is prior to all control and self management. One discovers that one identifies with sinners, and helpless and broken people, or one does not. If one does discover it, one knows from whence it comes, and one is grateful beyond measure for the glimpses into the Christ reality in others that have brought it about.

However, an important qualification must be added here. As darkness and emptiness in prayer may be a sign of a *passing over* from self to God, and the creation by God of the space within which we can work our transformation without hindrance, so it must often be in matters of personal relating. To see little or nothing of God or the form of Christ in another person is likewise an invitation by God to enter into the obscurity of real faith and to extend such faith to the area of charity. That the form of Christ is somehow and to some real degree in the other is quite beyond doubt. Not to see it is not necessarily a spiritual defect in the relationship. The deeper Christian meaning of loving others is perhaps more in place in such a situation, which *feels* all wrong and is full of mutual opaqueness, than when one is responding to what one sees with some clarity. What we have said about prayer so far in our reflections applies equally to life with others. It is only from a perspective which has its ultimate basis in faith that other persons will be rightly, even if darkly, seen.

What we have said has been said by way of encouragement, and as an attempt to indicate in a very brief and sketchy manner how St John of the Cross can be a source of light in the apparent (and unchosen) darkness of so many lives. All of the above may also be viewed as a commentary on the profound words of Karl Rahner.[8]

---

8   Karl Rahner, *Theological Investigations*, Vol 3, The Theology of the Spiritual Life, Darton, Longman and Todd, London, 1974, p. 89f.

John Welch O.Carm.

TRANSFORMED HUMANITY AND ST JOHN OF THE CROSS

The language of John of the Cross is bold. He bluntly states that through the purification of the dark night we are so transformed that *we become God*. For John, authentic human development is ultimately divinisation. He grants that creatures never become un-created, but the union is such that language of divinisation is appropriate. This chapter addresses the following questions:

What does it mean to be divinised?
What does it look like?
What are the qualities?
Is divinisation rare?

Sometimes in reading John of the Cross with his language of nada, stillness, solitude, one might assume that the contemplative is becoming more and more withdrawn and ends up catatonic in the corner. There used to be a stereotypical look that was associated with holiness. It was described this way: you knew a person was holy when she held her head at ten after six, and looked like she had just received bad news that the rest of us had not yet heard.

John describes the goal of the Christian journey in particularly lyrical terms in *The Living Flame of Love*, both in the poem and the commentary, and there finds words for his experience of divinisation or deification. He describes an intensely personal, intimate love relationship between the soul and God, a profound union in the very core of his being. John's description can lead to the question: What has happened to one's humanity under the impact of God's love?

Enslaved heart

One way of approaching the question is to ask: what is happening to the heart on this journey? John observed that the desires of the heart are restless, pulling us now here, now there. They are like little children calling for attention, and will not be still for very long. He noticed that even when the heart achieved something it deeply desired, it was satisfied for only a while, and then desires once more began tugging at the heart. John likened the condition to the situation of a lover who eagerly anticipates a special day with the beloved, and it turns out to be deeply disappointing. Our deepest desires relate us to God. John says simply, 'The soul's centre is God'.[1]

---

1   John of the Cross, The Living Flame of Love, in *Collected Works of
     St John of the Cross*, Kieran Kavanaugh OCD and Otilio Rodriguez
     OCD, Institute of Carmelite Studies, Washington DC, 1979, 1,12.

But as the heart gropingly reaches out for a God it often cannot name, the heart continually gives itself away to what is not God. In seeking the fulfilment of its desires our heart continually asks other people or possessions to quench the desire.

The heart asks a part of God's creation to be ultimate, to be God. The heart creates idols, and in giving itself to these idols, in centring its life around them as though they were God, the heart becomes enslaved. It is no longer free to respond to the invitation coming from the gracious presence at the centre.

That the heart loses itself this way seems to be an inevitable condition, and one difficult to treat. St Francis de Sales wrote that 'The diseases of the heart as well as those of the body, come posting on horseback, but depart slowly and on foot'.

Liberated heart

John urges an ascetical freeing of the heart. But in his own situation he reports that he could not loosen his grasp of that to which he was clinging. John learned that only God's love could entice him from his idols. Right where his desires were exhausting themselves trying to find fulfilment, in the dark of his apparent failure, John experienced a kindling of a deeper love. This love invited him past his deteriorating situation; it re-ordered his other loves; and it allowed him to slowly relax his grasp on his life and continue his life's journey in trust.

John helpfully points to signs which, when present in our lives, indicate powerlessness to control our own existence any longer; he encourages us to go into the night with patience, perseverance, and trust. This night, he learned, is a loving experience of a God who is healing the heart and transforming our desires.

Becoming God

John reports a remarkable transformation of his heart's desire as a result of surrendering to God in his soul's centre. John's desire and God's desire have now joined in a consonance of desires. John writes: 'What you desire me to ask for, I ask for; and what you do not desire, I do not desire, nor can I, nor does it even enter my mind to desire it. My petitions are now more valuable and estimable in Your sight, since they come from You, and You move me to make them...'[2] Again, 'This feast takes place in the substance of the soul ... thus all the movements of this soul are divine. Although they belong to it, they belong to it because God works them in it and with it, for it wills and consents to them'.[3]

John is reporting a remarkable transformation of our humanity. When we love on the merely sense level we love in a disordered way which turns everything back towards us and our immediate gratification. We love in a way which seeks our fulfilment, our happiness, our satisfaction.

Through a healing night, which John calls the night of the senses, an order is brought into our loves. In John's language the sense faculties and the spiritual faculties are now in harmony; we love in a more thoughtful and responsible manner. Now I do not love simply because the object

2   *The Living Flame*, 1,36.
3   *The Living Flame*, 1,9.

of my love satisfies me, but because it is the Christian thing to do. I can choose to love even when there is no immediate satisfaction.

But John reports an even further transformation. Through a deeper healing of an experience which he called the night of the spirit, a time when our knowing and loving is darkened and we proceed in a naked faith, the intention for our love seems to pass from us to God. We no longer have the reason for our love. The intention, the motivation for our love is now in God, and all we can do is love.

The soul and God are now so united, and there is such a consonance of desires, it is as though God were loving God in our love, as though God were loving God's world in our love, and all we can do is love in the world in a way which is loving. And the motivation essentially is no longer in us. John writes, '. . . the soul here loves God, not through itself, but through [God]'.4

Living without a why

Meister Eckhart, a 14th century Dominican, gives us further descriptions of a divinised person. Eckhart believed that detachment was the greatest of virtues, and the ultimate detachment would be to learn to live without a 'why'. Eckhart speaks of an inner place, similar to John's substance of the soul, where 'God's ground is my ground, and my ground is God's ground... It is out of this inner ground that you should perform all your works without asking, *why*'.5 Eckhart continues, 'So long as you perform

4   *The Living Flame*, 3,82.
5   Edward College OSA and Bernard McGinn, trans and intro, *Meister Eckhart*, Paulist Press, New York, 1981, 183.

your works for the sake of the Kingdom of heaven, or for
God's sake, or for the sake of your eternal blessedness, and
you work them from without, you are going completely
astray... Whoever is seeking God by "ways" is finding
"ways" and losing God, who in ways is hidden. But
whoever seeks for God without ways will find him as he
is in himself, and that man will live with the Son, and he
is life itself. If anyone went on for a thousand years asking
of life: "Why are you living?" life, if it could answer, would
only say: "I live so that I may live". That is because life
lives out of its own ground and springs from its own
source, and so it lives without asking why it is itself living.

'If anyone asked a truthful man who works out of his
own ground: "Why are you performing your works?", and
if he were to give a straight answer, he would only say, "I
work so that I may work"'.[6]

Apparently in this state of detachment, or in John's
condition of a union so profound that John speaks of God
loving in his love, a person is functioning in total accord
with his or her creatureliness.

Harmonious humanity

Is this divinised, detached person living as an automaton?
Has the Holy Spirit so taken over the personality that the
person no longer has to reflect and make decisions? It does
not seem that John became robotic. He reports that his
intellect is functioning but now in a divine way, and so
forth with his memory and will. The intimacy with God
apparently allows a person to function in a beautifully

6   *Meister Eckhart*, 183,4.

human way; and that human way of functioning, of knowing and loving, is now in total accord with God's will, with God's knowing and loving this world. Through the loving union with God the person is free to be the creature God created. John believed that the world is only truly known in God. As a result of this union a person's reading of the world would be much more in accord with God's view, and the decisions one makes would now be more in accord with God's love for this world. If we understand God's will for this world as the well-being of humanity, then the divinised person lives a life which is naturally co-operative with God's Kingdom. Their very life furthers a world of love, of justice, of peace.

Difficult to recognise

Are there many persons such as John is describing? It would seem they would be difficult to recognise. They are not living in a manner which would draw attention to itself. John's words indicate that this divinised person is extraordinarily integrated, living in her or his nature at such a level that their ordinary functioning is uniquely attuned to God's love of this world. Meister Eckhart says of those living without a 'why': 'But note, you must pay heed, for such people are very hard to recognise. When others fast, they eat, when others watch, they sleep, when others pray, they are silent − in short, all their words and acts are unknown to other people; because whatever good people practise while on their way to eternal bliss, all that is quite foreign to such perfected ones'.[7]

---

7   Richard Woods OP, *Eckhart's Way*, Michael Glazier, Wilmington, Delaware, 1986, 146.

Now, many of us fit this description. When others are fasting we are eating, when they watch in vigil, we are asleep, when they pray, we are silent. Obviously, it must take a keen eye to discern those who are living without a 'why' and those of us living without a clue.

An example

One of the most concrete descriptions of this state of intimate union with God, John's 'divinisation', is found in the writings of Teresa of Avila. In describing her situation in the seventh dwelling place in her *Interior Castle*, the situation of the mystical marriage, Teresa reports these effects:

- She has a deep union with God, but God does not preoccupy her. She goes about her business and is busier than ever.

- She learned to forget herself. She found that if she took care of the things of God, God would take care of the things of Teresa.

- She has a great desire to suffer, but she is not as hard on herself as previously.

- She no longer wants to die and be fully with God. She realises the question is, 'What does God want?' The purpose of prayer, as she always taught, is conformity with God's will.

- She reports a deep interior joy when persecuted, and has great compassion on her persecutors.

- She wants to either be alone, or serving souls.

- She no longer experiences dryness in prayer, and she rarely has ecstatic experiences anymore. Those occurrences were apparently part of getting acclimated to God.

- She concludes by warning her nuns not to build castles in the air. This loving condition they are in manifests itself in concrete care of the ones with whom they live and for whom they are responsible.

Summary

The divinised person appears to be one who is truly alive, whose powers have been actuated. The person will not have abilities they did not have before (such as suddenly playing the piano), but they will be free to use the gifts they do have.

The whole personality has been brought into harmony with its centre. It no longer wars against itself, operating in a dysfunctional manner. The divinised person is integrated, to the extent it is possible within the givens of any one life.

Because this person is knowing this world with God's knowing, and loving it with God's loving, he or she can be passionately related to this world, be committed to it, without the heart being fragmented or enslaved, and without distorting the world. This person loves with a freedom of spirit, without clutching.

Are there many people in this condition? Remembering Eckhart's warning that they are hard to spot, it is possible to guess that there are many 'divinised' people in our lives. John of the Cross said that with even one degree of love one is in the centre, but there are other centres within the centre and one can go deeper in God. I take this to mean that this divinisation is a process, a journey with many stages, always a pilgrimage.

Who is even fully alive, fully integrated, completely rooted, centred, fully self-possessed, completely free and undefended, totally self-giving? But who does not have some freedom, some generosity?

Maybe the flame of our spirit and the flame of God's Spirit are not one flame yet, but in their dance they touch one another, and go apart, they flicker within one another, they sometimes are lost within one another. John of the Cross says we are becoming God through participation in God, and he invites us to give ourselves over to the flame without fear, but with patience, perseverance, and trust.

Sonia Wagner SGS

WOMEN AND PRAYER

St John of the Cross and night: a feminist perspective

In his teaching on the dark night of the soul St John of the Cross provides guidance and encouragement today for many Christian feminists who so often experience frustration and what Constance Fitzgerald[1] refers to as '*impasse*' in the face of apparent institutional intransigence. This impasse flows over from experiences with institutional structures to touch relationships and especially relationship with God in prayer.

At the same time, John reminds those of us who might position ourselves at the other end of the spectrum from the feminists and who are likely to find change in the

---

1 Constance Fitzgerald, Impasse and Dark Night, in *Women's Spirituality*, Joann Wolski Conn, ed, New York, Paulist, 1986.

Church not too slow but rather too rapid, to lean only on the secure insecurity of dark faith.

He points out to all of us no matter what position we take in regard to our prayer life in the context of Church today that we can never afford to become fixated on anything less than God since the reality of God always surpasses our most precious images, dreams, preconceptions and programs. Our common mission is exploration into God, the focus and end of our prayer is God.

St John and the dark night

At the age of twenty-one John became a Carmelite and studied liberal arts and theology at the University of Salamanca. He excelled academically but his heart was not in it. He was not a scholar but a poet and a mystic. Unable to find an environment conducive to contemplation within the Carmelites he was considering leaving the Order and becoming a Carthusian. John was among the first Carmelite friars to accept Teresa's reforms and as a symbol of his commitment to a new and austere *discalced* way of life he changed his name to John of the Cross.

The first edition of his works appeared in Spain in 1618 under the title, *The Dark Night*. Perhaps this has contributed to the fact that the holy singer has been regarded as sad and full of suffering and this is especially connected with his prison experience. While there is little doubt that John's experience of prison had a profound effect on his understanding of darkness, he did not write the *Dark Night* in prison but in the midst of flowering nature, under the open sky. From prison comes the mystical love poem *The Spiritual Canticle*. His nine months in prison were not experienced by John as a time of meaningless darkness. He said that he composed *The Spiritual Canticle* under the influence of divine enlightenment and in an overflowing love despite his physical prison.

Suffering and our contemporary context

For many today the flood of overly optimistic spiritualities has failed to satisfy, precisely because they so often avoid engaging people on the level of their suffering. There is fresh understanding of our human need to find meaning in our suffering, to engage in the process of grieving if we are to be open to growth in the Lord. In fact we know that it is not possible to embrace tomorrow, to fully engage in the process of change if we do not grieve.

There is a great deal of suffering in our world. It extends from deeply personal and hidden domains through to social patterns and global realities. It even reaches cosmic dimensions. We go through precisely the same experiences in our relationships and our ministries as John describes regarding the soul's journey to God. We can read John and find encouragement that God is there in our own life, our relationships, our Church and our world.

In this dark age any spirituality that seeks to meet and speak to human experience must incorporate the fact and the meaning of suffering. W.B. Yeats[2] caught the truth present in pain in this way when he said that love had made its home in excrement, for, until love can be whole, it needs to have been tested.

2   William B. Yeats, Crazy Jane Talks with the Bishop, in *Oxford Anthology of English Poetry*, Tawry and Thorp, ed, 2nd edn, Oxford University Press, New York, 1956.

Dorothee Soelle[3] has written, concerning feminist theology, that all true theology begins in pain. Surely that is the reality for all theology. It is the reality of concrete pain known in the specific life situation of a person or a community which is the locus of faith. It is there that death is to be faced in anguish and there that life is strangely given.

Schillebeeckx[4] asserts that the most telling experiences culminate in our accounts of pain and suffering.

The authority of experiences therefore culminates
in stories of pain and misfortune and failure:
suffering pain, suffering in evil and injustice
suffering from and in love,
suffering over guilt. The deepest experiences
that guide our life are experiences of conversion...
a change of action, of mind and being.

Yet, it remains true, for most of us as we experience suffering, rather than feel a touch of God, we frequently tend to feel abandoned by God, rejected by God.

It can be argued that a theological reading of the history of Jesus, especially the story of the crucifixion, reveals the grief of God in the death of Jesus, the suffering of God in the suffering of the world. To attribute suffering to God using biblical sources certainly reverses our human categories, and it is difficult to think of God as participating in suffering, death and grief of the world. Applied to God the term is, of course, strictly metaphorical. The cross is a central Christian symbol and an important one for

3   Dorothee Soelle, *The Strength of the Weak*, Westminster Press, Philadelphia, 1984, p. 90.
4   Edward Schillebeeckx, *On Christian Faith: The Spiritual, Ethical and Political Dimensions*, Crossroads, New York, 1987, p. 127-8.

Christian women who experience the pain of exclusion and denigration in their own religious heritage.

It has been said that in a special way today women take part in the salvation of the world which God works out through the suffering of the just at the hands of the unjust. They do not suffer at the hands of a neutral power but at the hand of the Church they love.[5]

Impasse

I have chosen to speak of suffering in this context as impasse. By impasse is meant that there is no way out, no way around, no rational escape from what imprisons us. There is no possibility. All the normal escape hatches are no longer working. Impasse is experienced not only in the problem itself but also in any solutions that have normally been tried and found effective in the past. It is depletion. It presupposes limits. It is unavoidable suffering. An apt symbol for it is physical imprisonment – an experience of being squeezed into a confined space. All next steps are cancelled. A very real temptation is to give in to cynicism and despair in the face of disillusionment, disenchantment and loss of meaning.

It is the striking awareness that our categories do not fit our experience that throws the intuitive self into a quest for new possibilities. The pain can sometimes provide for the 'imaginative shock' necessary. The situation of being helpless can be efficacious. While nothing seems to be moving forward one can in fact be on a homeward exile.

5   Sandra Schneiders, *Women and Power in the Church: A New Testament Reflection*, Proceedings of the Catholic Theological Society of America 37, New York, 1982, p. 127-8.

For many women it is a dark night time of crisis and transition, both individually and collectively. It is a shadow time. Shadows can have several meanings for us as symbol. They refer to the shadows cast by our human structures and institutions, the difficulties, the problems and the obstacles. But shadows also denote, in the Jungian sense, the hidden potential, the unexplored possibility.

Women are not alone in their experience of darkness. Their experience relates them in solidarity to the poor, the weak and the marginalised of the world whether they be women or men.

The impasse that women report in relation to Church life is threefold. It involves a lack of understanding on the part of the institutional Church, sometimes not being taken seriously and frequently not being able to participate fully in the decision making processes of the Church.

While in impasse we experience powerlessness. This powerlessness can prove to be very powerful. Elizabeth Janeway[6] refers to the potentially world-transforming steps that constitute what she calls the *powers of the weak*. She names these power as disbelief, bonding and action in solidarity.

Spirituality

I am interested in how this marginalisation, subordination and exclusion in church and society has affected women's sense of themselves in relation to God. Let us now turn to the less public sphere of women's spirituality, namely

6   Elizabeth Janeway, *The Powers of the Weak*, Alfred A. Knoph, New York, 1980.

their experience of God. Spirituality is grounded in experience and story. It is lived faith. All of us are mystical people – fundamentally God-targeted and God-touched. Rahner says that the Christian of the future will either be a 'mystic' one who has experienced something or the person will cease to be a person at all.[7]

Women's experience in spirituality has some notable characteristics.

(a) Predominance of masculine experience

There has been a predominance of masculine experience on women's spiritual formation. What has been proposed for women has been a combination of masculine spiritual practice and the ideal 'eternal feminine' which is more a projection of the male 'anima' than a real ideal for women. Men have taught women to beware of specifically male vices: pride, aggression, disobedience to lawful hierarchical authority, homosexuality, lust and the like. Women have rarely been alerted to those vices to which their socialisation prompts them, e.g. weak submissiveness, fear, self-hatred, jealously, timidity, self-absorption, small-mindedness, submersion of personal identity and manipulation.

One of the problems about the traditional ideal of self-denial is that it has been applied unequally to men and women. Self-denial has been seen as the antidote to human pride... But the 'original sin' of women is not pride but passivity: abdication of their responsibility for themselves and allowing others to act upon them and for them.

7   Karl Rahner, *Theological Investigations, Vol 1*, 7, Darton Longman & Todd, London, 1974, p. 15.

The fundamental fallacy of the misuse of self-denial is that persons, especially women, have been called on to deny what they have not had the opportunity to affirm, to give up what they have never owned: a true sense of self.[8]

St John of the Cross maintains the primacy of relationship and surrender and yet teaches, too, the necessity of free choice or self-directed action and autonomy. It is important for women to know that God affirms their self-direction as well as their self-surrender. Religious belief and self-esteem are not incompatible. Autonomy has seldom been encouraged for Christian women.

Maturity is the result of developmental phases which require love even in darkness, loneliness or misunderstanding. This lack of consolation which throws us back on our own inner resources is, I believe, the path to autonomy (our contemporary term) or in classical terms persevering fidelity to one's inner calling.

(b) The predominance of the intellectual over the affective

The predominance of the intellectual over the affective approach to the knowledge of God, of method over intuition in prayer, of warfare over friendship as the model of the spiritual life, of asceticism over mysticism, of submission to authority rather than freedom in personal initiative have all expressed the concerns of men and the experiences of men. Women have been encouraged to be virile, soldiers of Christ.

8   Carolyn Osiek, *Beyond Anger*, Paulist Press, New York, 1986, p. 21.

Another aspect of the impasse is the austerity in modes of expressiveness that is encountered so often in church in Australia. As Bruce Dawe says *to speak what is in the heart is some dishonour.* The emotional key of the church life often lacks enthusiasm, and beauty in word and gesture is often absent. *There is no woodenness like Australian woodenness,* says Tony Kelly. *We have stiffened into stone and creaking wood.*[9] Perhaps the matter could be most effectively expressed in terms of the repression of the feminine in a very masculine Church.

(c) Eclipse of the feminine experience

An effective of male dominance in the area of spirituality has been the partial eclipse of the feminine experience and feminine models in Scripture and in the history of spirituality. How often when we retrace salvation history do we include not just Adam but Eve, not just Abraham but Sarah, not only Moses but Miriam, not only David but Ruth, not only Peter but Mary Magdalen? The only feminine model who has been invoked with real fervour and consistency has been Mary, the Mother of Jesus.

In our day the spiritual giants are at last being recognised and cooperatives and collectives of women are sharing wisdom in new and creative ways. We have fewer records of women saints partly because men have set the criteria for holiness and written the bulk of the accounts of lives judged holy.

9   Tony Kelly, The Church's Mission in Australia, in *The Church's Mission in Australia*, Mary Rose MacGinley PBVM and Tony Kelly CSsR, CollinsDove, Melbourne, 1985, p. 55.

(d) Impasse in language and imagery

Women often experience an impasse in regard to language and imagery for the divine. Celie in Alice Walker's novel *The Color Purple* experiences liberation from her oppression in the recognition of just how powerful and controlling languages and imagery have been in their relationship with God.[10]

Significant developments

While women have been conditioned to evaluate anything in their spiritual experience that seemed especially feminine as questionable or negative, there have been some significant developments. We have come to look with a critical eye on a spirituality that denies the body, is overly methodical, highly verbal and intellectual and over-emphasises the vertical dimension.

Now it seems that far from being neglected and under-valued some so-called feminine elements in spirituality interior silence, body-centred prayer, patience with oneself, compassion for others and intuition are now emerging as desirable.

Women are realising that though there has been impoverishment for them in the area of prayer and spirituality, this impoverishment can have some positive effects. In the process of growing maturity each person has the task of integrating his or her conscious ego with material from the unconscious. To achieve wholeness a person must integrate

---

10   Alice Walker, *The Colour Purple*, Harcourt Brace Jovanovich, New York, 1982, pp. 164-8.

the contra-sexual side of his or her personality. The woman must integrate the masculine. The man must integrate the feminine.

Women have always been taught to acquire masculine virtues and to think and pray in masculine ways. God has been imaged in masculine terms. On the other hand, men have been trained to repress and regard as shameful the feminine in themselves. Women may well have to work hard at fully appreciating themselves as feminine, but after all it is our own identity we are striving to understand and claim. The task is to come home to ourselves as women. Men, it seems, have the more difficult task of reversing the negative judgment on the feminine in themselves and then incorporating it into their personality.

Another effect of the masculinising of women's spiritual experience is that women often understand men's spiritual experience better than men understand women's. There has been a vast increase in the number of spiritual directors who are women. Women have a variety and depth of inter-personal experience welcomed and valued by many people and in the private sphere have developed some quite singular skills welcomed by many people.

To experience self as not among the godlike is in itself a call to both faith and humility. At least women have never taken it upon themselves to persecute others in the name of God. Women may have been burned as witches but rarely have they fought holy wars to defeat God's enemies.

The fact of being dependent on men for official religious participation has led women to specialise in the area of personal prayer for which they need no permission and find helps in the most unexpected places. Their suffering has been a fire in which much gold has been refined. Through a steady flow of stories, documents, papers and actions, women testify that they have discovered that male domination and the submission of women is a sign of personal and social groaning. This is brought about, according to the feminist perspective, not by God's original design for creation, but by human disobedience and dislocation.

Prayer

In the books of *Night/Ascent* John focuses on prayer, because ultimately night is about God working salvation and it is in prayer that it stands most defined.

Christian life has at all times been marked as a life of prayer. For long centuries a life of prayer has been seen as a withdrawal from human affairs and the dilemmas, tragedies and responsibilities of daily life in the marketplace. That is clearly not the kind of prayer called for in today's society, even among contemplative communities. Our love of God expressed in prayer does not require us to evade social responsibility. Far from it! It must flow into loving care of the most needy. Prayer has a dynamic function: to give rise to a more completely less exclusive or selective loving activity in the world.

Prayer and empowerment

Prayer, it has long been said, has four functions. Adoration, thanksgiving, contrition and petition. That is true but the first purpose of any intimate conversation is to get to know the Beloved better and in the very dynamic one gets to know self better. We begin to see things differently. The result of a loving mutual relationship is empowerment and liberation. Prayer has a critical function. It is that encounter with God, that surrender to God's word in which we are strengthened and steadied to see the world as it really is. It is the function of prayer to enable us to see prophetically, to be prophetic, and to act prophetically, to look at our world and ask the questions, 'What is there that should not be there? What is not there that might be there?' It is my understanding in reading St John of the Cross that for John not every suffering or experience of impasse is night. Not any suffering *is* night but any suffering can *become* night. For it to be night there must be:

an inflow of God's love and life;
a distaste, a reversal, a going backwards;
an openness of faith – bringing one's will into line with God.

In the contemplative night it is God's inflow, shifted to a deeper level, that causes the distaste at more accustomed levels. But elsewhere John widens the vision. His God is an inflowing God who will not fail to enter and transform where the caverns of the heart have been widened.

In his letter and the shorter works (*Precautions*) John uses the same language as he uses about prayer in *The Dark Night* to diagnose what is taking place in very human circumstances: the loneliness of leaving a loved community, being misjudged by superiors, let down by friends, material poverty, friction in community life, life's non-eventfulness.

. . . his Majesty has done this, to bring you greater profit . . . for the more he wants to give, the more he makes us desire, till he leaves us empty in order to fill us with blessings. . . . For this reason, the Lord would love to see her, since he loves her well, well and truly alone, intent on being himself all her company. . .

And your Reverence will have to stir yourself to be content only with his company, in order to find all contentment in it; for even if a person is in heaven, if she doesn't align her will to want it, she will not be content . . . [11]

(to Leonor, sent to a community in which she felt lonely).

All these are experiences which need to be corrected and seen differently in a faith perspective so that ultimately they might fit into God's caring plan of paradox and transformation. Experiences like these have the potential to ready the person for God's transforming gift. It is possible to view John's night in this way. His night it seems took place not in some lofty and mystical corner but in being physically and emotionally wrecked in prison. The work is done most powerfully, what just should not happen happens. It is then that faith, hope, love – as placing our meaning, security, affective centre in nothing other than God – is really expanded.

The dark night and contemporary application

Three things in particular entitle us to expand the scope of what John perceives in an intense form in the mystical dark night of the soul to have reference on a broader plane to our experience of Church and world.

First of all his insight begins in a poem. He confesses that his commentaries are only one exposition of that poem, which contains more than his prose explains (see *Canticle Prologue*). The symbol of the night as the place

---

11   John of the Cross, Letter 14, in *The Collected Works of St John of the Cross*, Kieran Kavanaugh and Otilio Rodriguez, trans, ICS Publications, Washington DC, 1979, p.696.

where security is wrenched from us and in which his Beloved bestows himself, is John's gift to the Church, independent of the mystical application he makes in his prose.

Secondly, the prototype of night in John's sense is Jesus in his suffering and death on the cross (*2 Ascent* 7:711) John makes night as cosmic as the cross is.

Thirdly, in the *Living Flame* John has a more global view of night. Looking back from the summit he sees the journey as a single process. There he sees this purifying action by the Spirit as beginning in 'what people are normally used to suffering', 'the trials that ordinarily and humanly happen to all that live' (2.27), 'difficulties and disappointments arising from *the world* as well as emotional pain and dryness in one's relationship with God' (2.25 cf. 2.30).

The life of St John of the Cross can be characterised by a sense of speed. By this I do not mean hurry but a swiftness to give his life the fullness of meaning. The fact of haste does not mean that it is not important to lay stress on the gradualness of the process of transformation. He experienced a tension between dynamism and patience but manages to convey a balance between these two extremes. He points out that every day has to be fully utilised (the dynamism) and yet at the same time we have to realise that it is a process that takes time (the patience). The feminist movement gives voice to those same tensions and is often poised between urgency and gradual development. In situations such as these, St John of the Cross counsels both docility to the Holy Spirit and serious endeavour.

Pope John Paul II has emphasised a broad application of the concept of night in his letter *Master in Faith*: 'Physical, moral and spiritual suffering, like sickness – like the plagues of hunger, like war, injustice, solitude, the lack of meaning in life, the very fragility of human existence, the sorrowful knowledge of sin, the seeming absence of God − are for the believer all purifying experiences which might be called *night of faith'*.[12]

For John the night works transformation. It is the space through which the Spirit can bestow blessings and change. However, night is not night without the right response. He calls it letting oneself be carried by God. This can demand the utmost courage and commitment, resisting the slide into bitterness. Night is not just about learning to wait till what we want comes our way. It is about being so widened in the waiting that it changes our wanting. Of this I am sure. The world is not saved by attempting a reversal of roles or even some levelling out process. The aim is not equality in every respect. Rather, it involves treasuring the differences and investing them with equal value and mutuality of respect. It is not just women having a turn at what men have done but a new way of seeing, a feminine way of being world. It is the gospel paradox − if you want to grow up you need to become a child again. If you want to lead then you must learn to serve. The gospel paradox is behind John's night reversal, not just teaching the person to pray harder or minister less selfishly but involving the person herself in a total conversion expressed as transfer from sense to spirit.

It is necessary to avoid entering into competition for what has been seen as male prerogatives in a sinful history based upon bullying. It is necessary to discern new possibilities for quite different ways of social organisation, community structures and cooperation. This calls for more

12   John Paul II, *Master in Faith*, Institutum Carmelitanum, Rome, 1991, No 14, p. 22.

than determination and aggressive energy; it also calls for contemplative sensitivity out of which new configurations can be imagined.

Feminism, darkness and the future

Does the night suffered by women mean seeking feminism in the gospel so that the world will not be given just another mess but a gospel order? Finally, of course, the symbol of the cross is not the end point for Christian thought: the resurrection and the hope for the future that it entails is from God and in God as well. The God who is future is the God of resurrection faith. The future of God is an important theme with its categories of hope, promise and new and not yet, the realm that is to come.

The experience of Christian women looks to a future in which the Church will express in its life and practice the quality and full personhood of women as Christians. To see God as future, as ahead rather than above or over against our human and natural world, is a different perspective that helps women see the feminist dilemma in the church as a temporary one.

We can ponder that the future of humanity lies in the hands of the men and women who are strong enough to provide the coming generations with reasons for living and hoping. Jesus' image for the reign of God is the festive table to which all people are invited and welcomed as partners. The festive table breaks down the usual barriers and divisions between people. There are no separate tables in the kingdom. It is no longer gender or economic class or racial background that is the determining factor. Only one thing matters – the willingness to see the world and its

people with new eyes and an open heart. Christopher Fry,
I suggest, echoes St John of the Cross and his teaching on
darkness when he has a young soldier in his play *A Sleep
of Prisoners* speak these words:

Dark and cold we may be,
but this is no winter now.
The frozen misery of centuries
breaks, cracks, begins to move.
The thunder is thunder of the floes,
the thaw, the floods, the upstart
Spring.
Thank God our time is now
When wrong comes up to face us everywhere
— never to leave us —
Till we take the longest stride
of soul men ever took.
Affairs are now soul-sized.
The enterprise is exploration into God.[13]

13 Christopher Fry, *A Sleep of Prisoners*, Oxford University Press,
England, 1951.

Placid Spearritt OSB

EMPTY IN PURE NEGATION:
THEOLOGICAL AND PRACTICAL IMPLICATIONS OF TAKING GOD SERIOUSLY[1]

'Empty in pure negation' is a phrase I have picked out from the *Living Flame of Love* in the hope of setting a cat among certain pigeons that strut, in my opinion, a little too complacently about the lawns of contemporary theology and spirituality. One of the things I like about St John of the Cross is that he is an extremist, as everybody must be who takes God seriously. Justifying those claims should provide sufficient material for this chapter.

---

1   This chapter is largely a reading, with commentary, of selected passages from St John of the Cross' Exposition of his poem *The Living Flame of Love*. Page references are to Vol 3 of *The Complete Works of Saint John of the Cross*, tr. by E. Allison Peers, Vol 3, London 1953. Section references, unless otherwise indicated, are to paragraphs in the second redaction of the Exposition of Stanza 3.

The phrase 'empty in pure negation' comes in the exposition of the third stanza of the *Living Flame of Love*. The stanza is meant to be about the delights of the union which St John calls spiritual marriage. The soul is enlightened and set ablaze by lamps of fire, his poetic image for distinct knowledge and love of the various infinite attributes of God, each of which is, as he says, 'the very Being of God in one sole reality' (3.2, p.145). 'The soul has become God of God by participation in him and in his attributes' (3.8, p.150; cf. 3.78, p.184).

God has given himself whole and entire to the soul. The soul is now in a position to give to God the only thing it possesses, which is God. 'And so at this time there is formed between God and the soul a reciprocal love in the agreement of the union and surrender of marriage, wherein the possessions of both, which are the Divine Being, are possessed by each one freely, by reason of the voluntary surrender of the one to the other, and are possessed likewise by both together, wherein each says to the other that which the Son of God said to the Father in St John, namely . . . All my possessions are thine, and thine are mine, and I am glorified in them' (3.79, p.185).

You see what I mean about extremism. You might very reasonably think we have jumped in at the deep end or, to change the metaphor, that this is rich food suitable perhaps for very advanced souls, but likely to cause serious spiritual indigestion to humble folk like you and me. However, you will recall that I said the stanza is meant to be about the delights of the spiritual marriage. In fact most of the exposition is devoted not to that elevated topic, but to the stage before that, namely spiritual betrothal, or more probably to the stage before that, the proximate preparation for spiritual betrothal. And that is a stage that will sound a whole lot more familiar to us lesser mortals, or at any rate to a good number of us.

The stanza in the poem is this:

Oh, lamps of fire, In whose splendours the deep caverns of sense which were dark and blind With strange brightness Give heat and light together to their Beloved! (p. 144).

The lamps are there all right, and their splendours cause the deep caverns of sense to produce light and heat and brightness; but the larger part of St John's exposition of the stanza is devoted to the preceding darkness and blindness of those caverns of sense. In that darkness and blindness you, probably, and I, certainly, will feel rather more at home.

The caverns are the faculties or powers of the soul, three of them in St John's Augustinian psychology: memory, understanding and will. They are very deep caverns: infinitely deep, for they can be filled with nothing less than the infinite God (3.18, p. 154).[2]

We are not normally aware that these three capacities of ours are infinite; and that is because they are not normally empty. 'For in this life any trifle that remains within them suffices to keep them so cumbered and fascinated that (neither are they) conscious of their loss nor do they miss the immense blessings that might be theirs, nor are they aware of their own capacity' (3.18 p. 154). Now there's an

---

2 Those of us who were brought up on a more purely Aristotelian-Thomist psychology have to keep in mind that memory here is more than sensory imagination, though even we Thomists carry an intellectual memory about with us, as well as the interior sense memory (cf. ST 1.79.6). Similarly, Thomists will have to remember that the other two caverns of sense are understanding and will, which in their vocabulary can only be senses in some very broad sense. (In ST 1.79.7 ad 1 St Thomas makes an interesting claim that St Augustine does not regard memory, intellect and will as three faculties. His reference is to De Trinitate 14.7, PL 42.1043.)

observation drawn from experience. We are accustomed to complain about people who play transistor radios all day long, that the constant trivial racket of bad music deprives them of the ability to appreciate either silence or good music, and further deprives them of any awareness of what they are missing. Well, it's true of the human spirit at prayer time too. If we grow accustomed to trivial thoughts and devotional exercises, we miss the immense blessings that might be ours, and begin to think of our powers, our faculties, as in fact finite. We tell ourselves that we are not capable of receiving the infinite God himself in our memory, our understanding and our will. That is bad theology and bad spirituality.

St John is dealing with a stage in the spiritual life of himself and of many whom he had observed, a stage in which they have been enlightened and purified (3.18, p. 154). The faculties are dissatisfied with the attractions of any or all created things; they hunger and thirst and yearn for God alone (3.19-21, p. 155). 'The spiritual appetite is empty and purged from every creature and from every creature affection' (3.18, p. 155).

Perhaps this state is fairly rare. There is another state, not unlike it, which is not rare: the state of a soul that continually falls for the attractions of creature affections, but is at the same time acutely and correctly aware that they are not going to satisfy its longings. Alcoholics would know this experience, but I suspect most, if not all of us, are dependent in this unsatisfying way on something or other.

Spiritual betrothal cannot take place until the soul 'is completely purged from all creature affection' (3.25, p. 157). Both in the state of betrothal (3.18, p. 154f, 3.26, p. 157), and in the proximate preparation for it (3.27, p. 157f), the soul experiences hunger and thirst and yearning for God to quite an intense degree (3.22, p. 155). The soul is not far from 'union with God and substantial transformation in all its faculties' (3.28, p. 158). Not far, but far enough to be acutely aware of its distance from its goal.

It is a delicate situation, in which it is possible for clumsy hands to spill all, to borrow a metaphor from the *Cloud of Unknowing* (chapter 34). Another powerful image for this critical stage in spiritual development is the story of the unfortunate Uzzah who put out his hand to the ark of God and took hold of it when the oxen stumbled; as though God were not capable of looking after himself without our assistance (cf. 2 Sam 6.6). It is of vital importance at this moment that the soul abandon itself to the leading of God, 'who will take it by the hand and lead it where it could not of itself go (namely, to the supernatural things which neither its understanding nor its will nor its memory could know as they are). Its chief care will be to see that it sets no obstacle in the way of him that guides it upon the road...' (3.29, p. 158).

Blind guides

There are, furthermore, three agents lying in wait ready to lead the soul astray precisely at this critical moment: three blind guides, 'namely the spiritual director, the devil and its own self' (3.29, p. 158f). Those blind guides will occupy much of our attention for the rest of this chapter, but first let me try to broaden the net so that what follows will catch rather more fish than those on the very brink of the spiritual marriage. St John expresses his anxiety 'to warn souls ... to take care what they are doing and into whose hands they commit themselves, lest they go backward...' (3.27, p. 157). And this warning he considers 'very necessary, not only for these souls that prosper on this way but also for all the rest who seek their Beloved' (3.27, p. 158).

So I think it fair to claim that his apprehensions about the blind guides might be relevant to any person who truly seeks God, at any point in the search, and particularly at any crucial turning point in the search.

I want also to claim that our particular time is one in which very large numbers of people are truly seeking God, expressing their hunger in reading books, listening to tapes, attending courses and seminars, going on retreats, joining prayer groups, searching out spiritual directors. There is a danger that such people will get so accustomed to searching that they forget that the object of the exercise is not to search but to find, not to travel but to arrive. A great deal of the spirituality on offer, much of it even on sale, is limited to everlasting preparation for something that never comes.

The purveyors of goods to this market would most of them baulk at the 'negative' flavour of the title of this chapter 'empty in pure negation'. I want to suggest that their very large quantities of 'positive' information and processes and techniques might actually hinder their customers from arriving at the God whose glory so transcends our limited minds that it is more accurately expressed in the emptiness of pure negation than in the plenitude of finite affirmation.

So let us turn to the three blind guides. St John seems to put them into a priority list, with the spiritual director first, the devil second, and the soul's own self third. He needs thirty-three paragraphs to warn us sufficiently of the dangers posed by the spiritual director; the devil can be dealt with in three paragraphs, and the soul itself in two. You may be able to guess which of the three will attract most of my attention. To leave room for him or her, let me take them in reverse order.

The soul

The main problem for the soul is that 'when God is pleased to bring it into that emptiness and solitude where it can neither use its faculities nor make any acts, it sees that it is doing nothing, and strives to do something' (3.66, p.178). We are dealing then with a devout soul that wants to pray but finds it can't. Its emotions are not stirred by holy thoughts, its mind won't stay on the job, its will runs all over the place. It is unable to produce good resolutions. It decides that nothing is happening. It goes along to its director or confessor and says it thinks it should be trying harder.

If its director is St John of the Cross he says how about not trying so hard? How about not trying at all? If you keep trying, he says, you are 'like a child whom its mother tries to carry in her arms, while it strikes out with its feet and cries out to be allowed to walk, and thus neither makes any progress (itself) nor allows its mother to do so' (3.66, p.178). We can leave the trying to God: he knows what's going on better than we do, and he's better able to control the process than we are. We don't have to be aware of progress; in spiritual matters it's better not to be self-conscious. So much for blind guide number three.

The devil

The second blind guide is the devil. The devil doesn't have too much scope with a soul that has become aware of its

own emptiness. His main job is to try to fill it up again
with the spiritual delights that God has emptied out, or
at least to bring enough of them back to mind to give the
soul something finite with which to busy itself. He likes
the soul to keep trying. 'For, it says, as it was doing nothing
in that solitude and quiet of the faculties, this other state
seems better, for now it is certainly doing something' (3.65,
p. 176). The devil likes people to be working seriously at
their spiritual life.

'For the evil one takes his stand, with great cunning, on
the road which leads from sense to spirit, deceiving and
luring the soul by means of sense, and giving it sensual
things, as we have said. And the soul thinks not that anything is being lost thereby, and therefore fails to enter into
the innermost chamber of the Spouse, but stands at the
door to see what is happening outside in the sensual part'
(3.64, p. 177). The only remedy against this busy curiosity
is again, to stop trying. 'If you are careful to set your
faculties upon naught soever, withdrawing them from
everything and in no way hindering them, which is the
proper part for you to play in this state alone, and if you
wait upon God with loving and pure attentiveness, as I
have said above, in the way which I there described
(working no violence to the soul, save to detach it from
everything and set it free, lest you disturb its peace and
tranquillity), God will feed your soul for you with heavenly
food, since you are not hindering him' (3.65, p.178).

The spiritual director

And so to the most troublesome of the blind guides. St
John of the Cross is not against spiritual directors, particularly for people who are beginning to take God seriously.

He is not against discursive meditation and emotional fervour in prayer, particularly for beginners. 'But when to some extent the desire has been fed, and in some sense habituated to spiritual things, and has acquired some fortitude and constancy, God then begins, as they say, to wean the soul and bring it into the state of contemplation, which in some persons is wont to happen very quickly, especially in religious, because these, having renounced things of the world, quickly attune their senses and desires to God, and their exercises become spiritual through God's working in them' (3.32, p. 159f).

Note the connection between the renunciation involved in prayer and that involved in the religious life. Both are of course extensions, or perhaps intensifications, or perhaps just particularly manifestations, of the renunciation required of anyone who would be a disciple of Christ: 'Whoever of you does not renounce all that he has cannot be my disciple' (Lk 14:33).

What St John of the Cross says about novices is no doubt true of anybody at, and for some time after, a moment of significant conversion to God or to Christ. At such a time the soul is capable of great generosity, willing and wanting to give up all possessiveness for the love of God. And God is not outdone in generosity.

Religious superiors and spiritual directors are apt to be suspicious of beginners who fly too high too soon. If the problem is visions and locutions and fervours they are right to be suspicious and discouraging. If the problem is simplification and quiet and emotional aridity and inability to meditate, if the novices are puzzled to find themselves not knowing quite what they want, but knowing they don't want to go back to the things they have given up, then I think the spiritual director and the religious superior had better examine themselves as possible candidates for the position of blind guides. There is no rule that says God is not allowed to give the grace of contemplative prayer to novices.

Passive contemplation

St John is talking about passive contemplation. 'God is the agent in this state and the soul is the recipient' (3.32, p. 160). At this point the earlier spiritual direction should go into reverse. 'If formerly (the soul) was given material for meditation, and practised meditation, this material must now be taken from it and it must not meditate; for, as I say, it will be unable to do so even though it would, and, instead of becoming recollected, it will become distracted' (3.33, p. 160).

'The soul has then to walk with loving advertence to God, without making specific acts, but conducting itself, as we have said, passively, and making no efforts of its own, but preserving this simple, pure and loving advertence and determination, like one that opens his eyes with the advertence of love' (3.33, p. 161).

This I believe is not an uncommon experience among people who take God seriously. Quite a lot of people find that at prayer time they don't want to be talking to God or making acts of devotion, but are content to receive what they are being given, like those that open their eyes with the advertence of love.

St John of the Cross makes a bold theological claim at this point: 'It is clear that if the soul at this time were not to abandon its natural procedure of active meditation, it would not receive this blessing (of communion with God) in other than a natural way. It would not, in fact, receive it, but would retain its natural act alone, *for the super-natural cannot be received in a natural way, nor can it have aught to do with it'* (3.34, p.161).

He is not denying the sacramental principle. He is not condemning creation spirituality. But he is saying that there is a movement in prayer that cannot be produced by the human spirit, a movement that comes exclusively from the spirit of God. St Paul, I think, agrees with him: 'We do not know how to pray as we ought, but the Spirit himself intercedes for us with sighs too deep for words' (Rom 8:26).

If it's true, it's a truth that was much neglected in theology and in spirituality at the time of St John of the Cross, and it is much neglected today. There is a movement in the life of prayer that is not subject to the judgment or to the direction of any authority on earth. Appeals to the inspiration of the Holy Spirit can be and are abused. But *abusus non tollit usum.* By their fruits you shall know them. If the soul that feels moved by the Spirit is judged – by others – to be at peace with itself and in charity with the rest of the world, we need to be very wary of casting stones.

St John of the Cross continues: 'it follows that ... this soul must be quite annihilated in its natural operations, disencumbered, at ease, quiet, peaceful, serene ... therefore the soul must be attached to nothing – to no exercise of meditation or reasoning; to no kind of sweetness, whether it be of sense or of spirit; and to no other kind of apprehension' (3.34, p.161). It 'must forget even the practice of that loving advertence of which I have spoken, so that it may remain free for that which the Lord then desires of it' (3.35, p.162).

This point I would regard as critical. We tend to think of the Christian obligation to love as an obligation to love *consciously*. The greatest of the commandments, and the second, which is like it (Mt 22:36-39) do not say we are to be *aware* all the time of loving God and neighbour. Loving God with all your mind does not mean thinking consciously about God all the time. That would be a very mindless way of loving anybody. It means allowing infinite scope to the natural appetite of the mind for truth: not loving anything or anybody else with a disordered love, such as would clog up with the finite what has to be left empty to make room for the infinite.

God at work

St John of the Cross has experienced a kind of prayer where it is all right to forget about love for a bit. It's all right, because our understanding of love is very limited, and God is not at all limited. This is a kind of prayer where God is doing the work, and can do it without our even opening our eyes with a drowsy pleasurable advertence of love.

The soul is not necessarily aware of the blessing it receives in passive contemplation, but it is at least 'able to attain to a perception of estrangement and withdrawal from all things, sometimes more so than at others, together with an inclination to solitude and a sense of weariness with regard to all worldly creatures and a sweet aspiration of love and life in the spirit. And in this state anything that does not imply such withdrawal is distasteful to it, for, as they say, when a soul tastes of the spirit, it conceives a distaste for the flesh' (3.39, p. 164). Again, I believe this kind of dissatisfaction with creature comforts is not uncommon in our culture. It is at least worth asking with the help of St John of the Cross whether the people who attend conferences on his spirituality are not familiar with the sense of weariness he describes.

In our day and age, we are nervous of the dualistic distinction between the spirit and the flesh, in spite of our devotion to the scriptures from which the distinction comes (cf. e.g. Mk 14:38; Jn 6:63; Gal 5:16-25). So we spiritual directors would be for telling the disciple not to be withdrawing from the flesh, but rather to be facing up to it, working through it, affirming it.

Well St John of the Cross doesn't agree. He considers that under this 'distaste for the flesh' the soul is receiving inestimable blessings, 'the most secret and therefore the most delicate anointings of the Holy Spirit' (3.40, p. 164).

The spiritual director should on no account interfere with these workings of God. 'Although the gravity and seriousness of this evil cannot be exaggerated, it is so common and frequent that there will be found hardly a single spiritual director who does not inflict it upon souls whom God is beginning to draw nearer to himself in this kind of contemplation' (3.43, p. 165). Whenever this is happening, 'there will come some spiritual director who has no knowledge save of hammering and pounding with the faculties like a blacksmith . . . he will say: "Come now, leave these periods of inactivity, for you are only living in idleness and wasting your time. Get to work, meditate and make interior acts, for it is right that you should do for yourself that which in you lies, for these other things are the practices of illuminists and fools"' (3.43, p. 165). Brave words at a time when illuminists were being handed over to the secular arm for burning. We don't burn contemplatives in Australia today, but perhaps we continue to take them for deluded fools, and treat them accordingly.

'If one that has reached his goal begins to set out again for it, he is doing a ridiculous thing, for he can do nothing but walk away from it. When, therefore, through the operation of its faculties, the soul has reached that quiet recollection which is the aim of every spiritual person, wherein ceases the operation of these faculties, it would not only be a vain thing for it to begin to make acts with these faculties in order to reach this recollection, but it would be harmful to it, for it would cause it distraction and make it abandon the recollection that it already has' (3.44, p. 165f). Let us beware of the group leader who says, 'No you may not diverge from the approved method: you may not sit quiet in the back row when we're all holding hands and singing Alleluia: you may not cease repeating the mantra: you may not stop using the rosary'.

Empty in pure negation

'Let them (spiritual directors) strive to disencumber the soul and to set it in a state of rest, in such a way that it will not be bound to any particular kind of knowledge, either above or below, or be fettered by covetousness of any sweetness or pleasure or any other apprehension, but that it will be *empty in pure negation with respect to every creature* and will be established in poverty of spirit. It is this that the soul must do as far as in it lies, as the Son of God counsels, in these words: "He that renounceth not all the things that he possesseth cannot be my disciple" (Lk 14:33)' (3.46, p. 167).[3]

Empty in pure negation, not bound to any particular kind of knowledge of things above or of things below: this

---

3   The thought and the imagery are not very different in the first redaction: For when it is detached from all knowledge of its own, and from every desire and all affections of its sensual part, and dwells in the pure negation of poverty of spirit, wholly emptied of the mists of sweetness, . . . it is impossible that God will not perform his own part (3.40, p. 74).

is a very extreme recommendation. In order to come to the fullest union with God that is possible in this life, a union he calls spiritual marriage, St John of the Cross is convinced that we need to renounce our grasp on all creatures, including our knowledge of things above. If we cling to holy thoughts in our prayer, then we shall impede the action of God in bringing us to 'the aim of every spiritual person, wherein ceases the operation of (our human) faculties' (3.45, p.166).

It is when St John of the Cross is recommending us to be empty in pure negation that he refers us to the most powerful of the renunciation texts from the four gospels, that of Luke, chapter 14, in which Jesus tells great multitudes of people (Lk 14:25), 'If anyone comes to me and does not hate his own father and mother and wife and children and brothers and sisters, yes, and even his own life, he cannot be my disciple' (14:26). 'Whoever of you does not renounce all that he has cannot be my disciple' (14:33). Perhaps we could translate, 'does not hate his ownership of father and mother . . . his ownership of his life. . . '.[4]

'This,' St John of the Cross goes on to say, 'is to be understood, not only of the renunciation of all temporal things with the will, but also of the surrender of spiritual things, wherein is included (attained?) poverty of spirit, in which, says the Son of God, consists blessedness' (3.46, p.167).

Note his interpretation. In religious life particularly but in Christian life generally we are agreed — at least theoretically — that it is good to renounce bad things. St John of the Cross is saying it is good to renounce good things too.

---

4   This renunciation is what John Follent in his chapter has called expropriation, and John Welch detachment.

We are agreed — theoretically — that it is good to renounce temporal things. He is saying it is good to renounce spiritual things too. Ultimately, it is necessary to renounce spirituality if we are to clear the decks to receive God, which after all was supposed to be the object of the exercise in the first place.

'When in this way the soul voids itself of all things and achieves emptiness and surrender of them (which, as we have said, it the part that the soul can play), it is impossible, if the soul does as much as in it lies, that God should fail to perform his own part by communicating himself to the soul, at least secretly and in silence. It is more impossible than that the sun should fail to shine in a serene and unclouded sky; for as the sun, when it rises in the morning, will enter your house if you open the shutter, even so will God, who sleeps not in keeping Israel, still less slumbers, enter the soul that is empty and fill it with divine blessing' (3.46, p. 167).

It is impossible that God should fail to perform his part. This is one of the theological propositions I particularly want to draw to your attention. So much popular spirituality, and the theology that implicitly underlies it, has God playing a cat and mouse game with the soul: you make this move, he'll do that. He jumps here or there to see which way you'll go. This is a puerile idea of God. There can be no such animal.

A more refined version of this language, betraying the same theological misunderstanding, often breaks out at the penitential rite at the beginning of Mass: God has given us so much grace — or worse still, so many graces: how have we responded to his grace? This is a kind of transactional or bartering spirituality that subjects God as well as the soul to the play of market forces.

St John of the Cross from the vantage point of his pure negation is able to see the elemental simplicity of a God who cannot abstain from giving all that he is to everyone: elemental simplicity and infinite gratuitous generosity. *Bonum est diffusivum sui,* in the words of Dionysius the Areopagite: the Good pours itself out. Our spiritual endeavour is to receive what is in any case being given: to quit occupying our infinite capacities with finite obstacles, including good obstacles, including spiritual obstacles.

Those who guide us then, should 'be content with preparing the soul for this according to evangelical perfection, which is detachment and emptiness of sense and of spirit; ... and since God is the supernatural artificer, he will build supernaturally in each soul the building that he desires, if you yourself prepare it and strive to annihilate it with respect to its operations and natural affections' (3.47, p. 167). If we are to try harder at anything in prayer, we are to try harder to stop trying so hard. The way to annihilate, to cut out the operations of our faculities and the wandering of our natural affections, is not to engage in hand-to-hand combat on their own ground, but to go for detachment and emptiness: to stop trying.

The soul 'would be making no progress if it were to understand anything distinctly. The reason of this is that God, towards whom the understanding is journeying, transcends the understanding and is therefore incomprehensible and inaccessible to it; and thus, when it is understanding, it is not approaching God, but is rather withdrawing itself from him. Therefore the understanding must withdraw from itself, and walk in faith, believing and not understanding. And in this way the understanding will reach perfection, for by faith and by no other means comes union with God; and the soul approaches God more nearly by no understanding than by understanding' (3.48, p. 168).

The understanding 'is voiding itself of all that it could apprehend, nothing of which could be God; for, as we have said, God cannot be apprehended by the soul' (3.48, p. 168).

As with understanding, so with the will. The soul 'must see to it that the will is empty and stripped of its affections' (3.51, p. 170). 'In order to journey to God, the will has rather to be continually detaching itself from everything delectable and pleasant than to be conceiving an attachment to it. In this way it completely fulfils the precept of love, which is to love God above all things; and this cannot be unless it has detachment and emptiness with regard to them all' (3.51, p. 170f).

In our natural operations, it is true that there is no love without understanding. In these supernatural operations of God in the soul, there is both understanding and love: but they are God's actions, and therefore seem general and dark to the soul, not clear and distinct. 'As (God) himself cannot be understood in this life, the understanding is dark, as I say, and after the same fashion is love in the will; although sometimes in this delicate communication God communicates himself more to the one faculty than to the other, and acts on the one more than on the other, the soul being at times more conscious of understanding than of love, while at other times it is more conscious of love than of understanding; at times, again, all is understanding, without any love, and at times all is love and there is no understanding' (3.49, p. 169).[5]

Once more, if the experience of St John of the Cross is reliable, it must be important for us not to try to be

5   All is understanding, without any love is the second redaction's stronger version of the first redaction's expression all is understanding, and there is hardly any love (3.43 p. 76).

conscious of love – least of all in the feelings, but not in the will either – if that consciousness does not come of its own accord. The fact that we are not aware of love does not mean that it is not there. At this stage of the spiritual life, it means that it is the love of God, filling the emptiness we have provided by renouncing our own finite attempts to love.

This long section of the exposition of *The Living Flame of Love* has concentrated on the damage done to souls at a particular stage of their spiritual development by spiritual directors who act as blind guides. St John continues to warn them and threaten them for several more paragraphs, and although he waxes fairly angry, his dominant concern is for the soul itself: 'For the business of God has to be undertaken with great circumspection, and with eyes wide open, most of all in a case of such great importance and a business so sublime as is the business of these souls, where a man may bring them almost infinite gain if the advice he gives be good and almost infinite loss if it be mistaken' (3.56, p.172f).

I am sorry to burden you with what will seem to many a very specialised matter affecting only one very special time in some people's spiritual development. My problem is that I agree with St John: it's a matter of almost infinite gain or loss. And I don't agree that it's relevant only to a few. I agree with St John that it is 'very necessary, not only for these souls that prosper on this way but also for all the rest who seek their Beloved' (3.27, p.158).